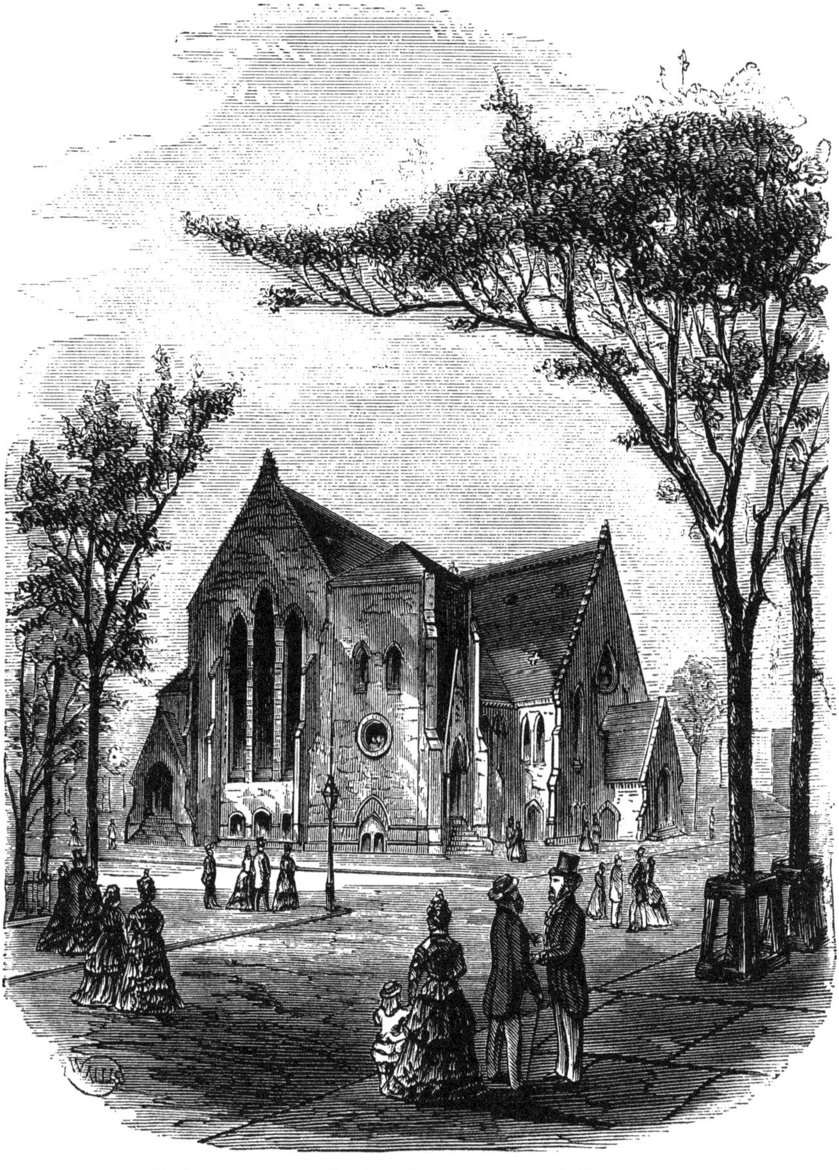

DAVID SWING'S CHURCH.

THE FOURTH PRESBYTERIAN CHURCH, COR. SUPERIOR AND RUSH STS.,

CHICAGO.

THE LAKESIDE PRESS, CHICAGO.

DAVID SWING'S

SERMONS.

Your friend
David Swing

CHICAGO:
W. B. KEEN, COOKE & CO.,
1874.

Entered according to act of Congress, in the year 1874, by
W. B. KEEN, COOKE & CO.,
In the office of the Librarian of Congress, at Washington.

CONTENTS.

PUBLISHER'S NOTICE.

This volume contains Fifteen of PROF. SWING'S very best discourses, all of which have appeared in "*The Chicago Pulpit*" and "*The Alliance*." Here may be found the celebrated Sermons, for utterances in which he was cited to appear before the Presbytery of Chicago, which will pass judgment upon the Orthodoxy of PROF. SWING, being impelled thereto by the charges of Heterodoxy against him, by Rev. Dr. Patton, a Presbyterian Theological Professor, and editor of *The Interior*.

The volume embraces Dr. Patton's charges against Prof. Swing, reprinted in full—also Prof. Swing's Declaration to the Presbytery at the commencement of his trial.

The following are the Sermons referred to particularly in Dr. Patton's specifications:

INFLUENCE OF DEMOCRACY ON CHRISTIAN DOCTRINE; SOUL CULTURE; A RELIGION OF WORDS; THE VALUE OF YESTERDAY; OLD TESTAMENT INSPIRATION; ON THE DEATHS OF CHIEF JUSTICE CHASE AND JOHN STUART MILL.

Chicago, May, 1874.

MARY PRICE COLLIER.

BY DAVID SWING.

Upon thy grave adorned with flowers sweet,
Whose leaves are bursting in this vernal air,
The stranger comes and drags inhuman feet
Across the tears and lilies mingled there.

The heart that moulders in that lowly bed
Shames the rude mortal on the clay above;
She followed only where her Savior led,
Her life no jarring discord, but a Love.

From wreath of girlhood to the snowy shroud,
The matchless beauty of that life to me
Spoke forth each day in accents deep, not loud,
And now comes back in holy memory.

The Christ unknown where dark accusing word
Fills God's own temple with wild, savage strife,
Burst from her heart, a music sweetly heard,
The Matin and the Vesper of her life.

They that have loved are they that shall not die,
Souls cold and harsh men hasten to forget,
The winter night comes soon, the summer sky
Beams on in Glory though its sun has set.

When times have come and times have gone again,
And God has called the unfeeling mind to rest
In grave unloved and all unknown of men,
Fresh tears will still be falling on her breast.

DAVID SWING'S SERMONS.

A BROAD ORTHODOXY.*

DAVID SWING.

To the intent that now unto the principalities and powers in heavenly places might be known by the Church the manifold wisdom of God.—*Eph.*, *iii: 10.*

The theme drawn from this text for your thought this morning is contained chiefly in the words "manifold wisdom of God." The other ideas of the passage may be alluded to after this one thought shall have been studied.

If, as some suppose, Christianity is to be all summed up in any one doctrine, then the Bible is an unusually large book for so simple a purpose. But if God has made the Church and the Bible a mirror in some sense of His vast and varied thought as to the duty and destiny of His children, then the Bible in its immense store of truth between Genesis and the Apocalypse is only a picture of the manifold wisdom of its author. Whoever reads the oracles of religion as contained in our Scripture must feel how fitted they are to the many forms of human want and character. If there are minds fond of symbols, they may find all through the Old Testament or in the vision of St. John a statement rendered almost wholly in the language of symbolism. When we remember the happiness and the knowledge which the buoyant, poetic years of youth reach through figures of speech drawn from the material world, we must rejoice that the book which is to influence their moral career is so full of figurative language from the Psalms of David to the last chapter in John's revelation. Although

*Sermon delivered in Fourth Presbyterian Church, April 26, 1874.

an immense amount of time and labor has been wasted over the effort to make literal prophecies out of John's poem and to find fulfillment along the path of history, yet, notwithstanding this long error, the poetic part of the world has extracted a great amount of good theology from those pages so terrific as to the wicked, so glorious as to the righteous. From that book comes the New Jerusalem, the White Throne, the River of Life, the Pearly Gates, the Crystal Sea. When we remember also what a multitude there is of less poetic and more formal minds, we feel the value of the great apostle who spoke always as a solid reasoner with definite premises and definite conclusions. In the world everywhere there is a group, more limited indeed, but powerful, who study questions of duty as between man and man, and man and God, and to these what an exhaustless fountain of thought is opened up in the sermons and words of Jesus. Here the Quakers exhaust their life and love. This many-sided wisdom of God has, however, another significance at which it is our purpose more particularly now to refer. There is a many-sidedness of doctrine just as marked as the variety of literary or logical style. We come along with our ardent desire to form a catechism or a formula that shall include and evermore contain the wisdom of God to men, but no sooner do we close up our estimate and prepare to rejoice over our work, than along comes some new student or some new age and reminds us of something important left out. In his history of Christian doctrine, Dr. Shedd alludes to perhaps a score of catechisms, all which sprang up within a small area of space, and all which compilations differed from each other. The variations of Protestants formed the theme of a long and once called powerful argument against the Protestant sect. So numerous had catechisms become before the day of John Knox, and as varying as numerous, that he announced when he published his that if any friends discovered some point wherein it seemed to come in contact with Scripture, he would change it in the next edition. This multiplicity of confessions of faith must descend from the fact that the study of God is too high and too broad for man, and that after his most patient effort he must sit down over the result saying, "Hast thou by searching found out God? Canst thou find out the Almighty to perfection?" And next to the infinity of God as rendering incomplete the theologies of men comes the wonderful scope of human want and character. There are myriads of hearts and myriads of minds, and large must be the volume of truth which shall offer food for all at all times. There have been timid, distrusting souls which have gone through life feeding all the way upon a score of truths culled from the Bible, which truths would have been of little price had they been repeated to the ear of the extreme egotist. There have been sorrowful souls, such as Cowper, and pensive souls, such as Fenelon, over which has daily passed like an autumnal sigh the breath of only a few sad doctrines, as if the gorgeousness of summer had gone by and nought remained but for her faded leaves to fall. When Maria de-La-Mothe read the Bible, she never passed away from the New Testament, and seldom from the story of Christ as related by St. John, for her religion being one of love to Christ, she passed her life where He was nearest in His words and character. For her, to live was Christ.

This immense scope of the Bible, and this similar breadth of human life, are facts which render it a vain attempt to gather up Christianity into a catechism, and thus treasure it up for ourselves and our children. A "Confession of Faith" can be only an imperfect index of the book. In some editions of Homer and Virgil there stands an argumentum at the head of each canto to tell us what the next thousand lines are all about; but, oh! how dead that statement is to the mind that knows what a world of beauty and sentiment, and of joy and suffering, is beyond, flashing in the sunshine of genius, and arrayed in the full verdure of the heart and the drapery of language.

When we behold the magnificence of the world and the greatness of man, and then turn also to the throne where He sits to whom earth and man are both as nought, we realize how vain must be the desire of the spirit to find some symbol in language which shall carry in it the meaning of the great book of religion lying open for the guidance and salvation of society. It is amid some of the manifold shadings of doctrine Paul stands in the letter to the Corinthians, and at the close of a most eloquent review he names three virtues, and then declares charity to be the greatest of the three. Whether it is the enthusiasm of the orator or the calm reason of the philosopher which speaks is uncertain, but this we know, that he places faith and hope both in the second place compared with the heart's love. It would seem to us un-Presbyterian in any way to slight the faith which has so covered itself with glory since the reformation, but who ever reads the Bible with any thoughtfulness will often find his favorite word quite overthrown and the substance of things put in its place. The worship of words is wonderfully overthrown in that book, and go to what term you please you will soon hear the commandment, "Thou shalt have no other gods before Me." No sooner have you concluded that there is nothing valuable but faith, than along comes the same Paul and says, "We are saved by hope;" and before your soul becomes fitted to this surprise, or can call a council together to announce "hope" as a *saving* doctrine, the same Paul has declared that charity is better than either hope or faith; and while you stand amazed amid these heresies, James comes along, and declares that "by works are ye saved."

Now these are not contradictory voices, but harmonious tones. Each one of these terms presents a phase of Christian experience. They are colors in a gorgeous moral landscape. As among the hills in autumn a company of rambling friends will say to each other, "What a blue in that sky! what a russet on that oak! what a crimson in those leaves! what a saffron here, what a purple there!" so in the words of God the free mind turning its pages must say, "What faith! what hope! what works! what baptism! there is in these rules of life and death." A faithful reading of the Bible is the death of all words worship. The life and salvation portrayed in it are so Godlike that they elude exact definition and pass and repass before us as the heavens move over us by night, with depths we cannot measure, and with stars we cannot count. Our books of doctrine are valuable as outline indices of a volume too large to be fully mastered or retained, but compared to God's word they are as a skeleton of the dead body compared with that body itself when, robed in beauty, it greeted its friends in the street or was the life of the sacred home.

The Immertionist is a person who sat down to read the Testament, and who came to four or five passages which informed him "that he that believes and is baptized shall be saved," but who paused before he came to the sixth statement, which would have omitted the immersion and have said, "He that believes shall be saved." The Solifidian is nothing but a Bible reader who, having found five texts that give salvation to faith only, went away and made up his creed without waiting for any remarks from any quarter about good works or immersion. The Fatalist is a mortal who has turned the sacred book over to find passages that should indicate the absolute empire of God and the abject humility of man, and fixing his whole gaze at last upon the figure of "clay in the hands of the potter," has announced the dogma "that man is predestined to his condition on account of nothing he has done or ever could do, but solely by the will of God;" while the Arminian is one who has read all such words as "come unto me," "seek and ye shall find," "whosoever will let him take the water of life freely." Hence, much of each creed is only an indication to the world as to what part of the Bible the makers of it had canvassed. When a ship anchors at New York, and begins to unload a cargo of oranges and pineapples, you perceive at once that that vessel does not come in from all nations, from Greenland and

England and Germany, but from some island or port in the Southern sea. It is thus in the world of theology. When you pick up a confession of faith of any Church and read a few pages, you perceive at once that the book has not come in from all the great Bible of the Almighty, but that this particular ship has received its cargo at Dort or Nice or Geneva. Far be it from you, I hope, to despise these human compendiums of truth, for a book is valuable if, in condensed form, it makes only a tolerable estimate of the divine truth; for going to the Bible yourself alone you would not be able to deduce so full or true a philosophy of life and salvation. When the Westminster assembly sat in council for four years, it is fairly presumable that they summed up the doctrines of the Bible, as would have been impossible to the world, that stood in vast multitude without. Hence it would be folly and vanity not to confess the value of their great digest. But after all this admiration, we know that creeds are not the places where divine wisdom fully expresses itself, but are the places where the hnman mind fails, places where the human mind gives up and seeks rest. The creed of the Immertionist only informs us where the student paused; and the creed of the Fatalist only tells us what verses he read. Thus all these compendiums are marks set up to tell us where the toiler quit work.

Do you recall to mind, my friends, how weary Dr. Chalmers became of these human forms in his later years? After he had preached his astronomical sermons, and had by scientific study begun to see how vast a thing the universe is, he seems to have outgrown the mediæval theology, and to have placed great stress upon the general but unpopular idea of being a good Christian. In Dean Stanley's "History of the Church of Scotland," the historian says, "Even late in life he, Chalmers, was accused by *suspicious zealots* of being an enemy to systematic theology, and his reply was certainly calculated to allay the alarm." I omit to reply. It was in brief that he preferred "the New Testament." Who those "suspicious zealots" were Dean Stanley does not state, and perhaps it would be impossible for any historian to separate their names from the oblivion which comes soon and deep to minds that are only "suspicious zealots" in the great battle of life.

The accusation brought about no reform, for in the debate over the "Sustentation Fund" Dr. Chalmers exclaimed, "Who cares about the Free Church compared with the Christian good of the people of Scotland? Who cares about any Church but as an instrument of the most Christian good? For, be assured that the moral and religious well being of the people is of infinitely higher importance than the advancement of any sect."

Chalmers in one of his broad discourses quoted this little fragment of verse:

"The man
That could surround the sum of things, and spy
The heart of God and secrets of His empire,
Would speak but love. With love, the bright result
Would change the hue of intermediate things,
And make one thing of all theology."

These thoughts and this poetry from Dr. Chalmers, too, in his glorious old age! It is not to be wondered at that under the leadings of such hearts the Free Church of Scotland sprang forward to a great career. His was not the only wide soul of that day. The almost equally great Dr. Duncan expressed ideas equally heretical and alarming. He said: "There is a progressive element in religion. It is a mistake to look upon our fathers as our seniors. They are our juniors. The Church has advanced wonderfully since its foundations were laid." * * * "I am first a Christian, next a broad Christian, thirdly a Calvinist, and fourthly a Presbyterian."

I have drawn these illustrations from history to remind you that the manifold glory of God is too varied and too vast to be caged up in the phrases of a few men at some given time and place. Say what we may in our condensed formulas, the glory of God will flash on in the New Testament as though we had taken nothing away from its profusion. Our creed is a few flowers plucked from the vast prairie between Lake Michigan and the Missouri.

After you have declared that one is saved by only the deity of Christ, I turn to the book of books and find the disciples all busy with His humanity alone. And after you have cried out "faith alone," I find Magdalen much forgiven because she had loved much, and Peter forgiven because of his tears of penitence, while the woman who emptied the alabaster box seemed blessed on account of her good works done in the name of Jesus. The truth is, salvation seems like the city of Thebes, entered by any one of a hundred gates, all beautiful portals of marble or bronze, or glittering brass, but all opening from the dreary, lonely country into the splendor of society and art and government. But come in by any gate, it was Thebes you perceived and reached. So in religion, be the golden gate, faith or hope, or charity, or penitence, or virtue, it opens out upon the presence of Christ. He must be the central object, the motive of the footstep, the vision before the eye, whether the eye is radiant with a saving hope or bedimmed with penitential tears.

Now we are informed in the text that the Church was organized to make known to principalities and power this many-colored wisdom of God. To the raptured vision of St. Paul, to his elevated mind, which never took a common view of any subject, but to which all the truths of religion loomed up toward the very throne of the Almighty, it seemed that the Church was established that it might unfold the glory of God before all the potentates of earth and heaven. So grand was this redemption of a world to be, that it seemed to Paul even the very seraphim in heaven would look down upon earth and see God's love pouring forth through Jesus Christ and flooding the earth, not in wrath as in the days of Noah, but with the windows of heaven open for a new outpouring—that of infinite grace.

As in presence, therefore, of an august company which Paul calls "principalities and powers," and to which we, less poetic, less divine, and more earthy, add the nations of the earth, the heathen world, the educated world, the skeptical world, as being the "principalities and powers" that plainly encompass us all—in such a presence, let us make the Church a place not where the narrowness and vanity of man are unfolded, but where all eyes looking may catch glimpses of the manifold wisdom of God. The manifold discords of man have already made sad havoc of this manifold wisdom of the Creator and Savior. The Church has been so narrowed that it would seem not ordained as a gate to heaven, but as a wall to keep the world away from its bliss. The principalities and powers looking down from heavenly places must see the tumults of sects rather than the sparkling sea of redeeming love. Oh, may these scenes hasten away from earth, and may the Church throw open all the gates of life, that future ages may see the world coming to salvation by many roads, some by faith, some by love, some by hope, some by charity, but all by the one Christ as He is freely offered to all in the Gospel.

INFLUENCE OF DEMOCRACY ON CHRISTIAN DOCTRINE.*

DAVID SWING.

One generation passeth away, and another generation cometh; but the earth abideth forever. *Ecclesiastes 1: 4.*

This verse from the Bible is read, not as a text out of which a discourse may be developed, but rather as a pensive thought, which suggests a line of reflection, perhaps beyond the meaning of Solomon, and hence beyond the warrant of the passage. All we claim for the words is that they invite the heart to mark how generations come and go, bearing away with them their customs and thoughts in part, and leaving the stage of action clear for a new scene. Paul also said, "The fashion of this world passeth away." Cicero said, "The times are changed, and we are changed in them." Paul in his Corinthian letter confesses that his teachings were modified by the times which he described as being a "present distress." The greatest Being of earth declared that some Mosaic customs were authorized on account of a local and temporary "hardness of heart." Thus by these voices, sacred and profane, we are reminded of the changes taking place in the internal and external appearances of society, in its dress, machinery, arts, beliefs, sentiments and hopes.

There are a few mortals who, by some strange fatality, have escaped learning this lesson of a changing world, and who are ready to denounce as infidel, the mind that presumes any part of the past to have become the subject of repeal. Antiquity is their test of truth.

From this bondage to that which has nothing to recommend it but its dust, the majority of the public, especially in cities, has escaped, and in their presence there is no longer need for proof that the times are always busy reshaping the ideas and the things of yesterday. The same activity and progress that are shaping the implements of industry and the material pursuits of men, are shaping also their thoughts, beliefs, motives and hopes.

*A Sermon preached by David Swing, in McVicker's Theatre, April 20, 1873.

The whole Mosaic economy was an adaptation of moral teachings to a particular condition, and hence, when the Saviour came, His first work was to remove ideas that had lived beyond their proper time. The law of eye for eye, tooth for tooth, the law of divorce, the law of caste, were all repealed or modified in answer to the demands of a new era.

We have thus the highest authority of a personal nature for confessing and expecting all the ideas of men to be modified, repealed or enlarged, by the influence of new times and places. To this authority of person, we add the facts of human life, which go to show that ideas are modified by climate, and government, and by the popular education. What has been useful in one age has been useless in another, not because the idea has ceased to be true, but because it has ceased to be pleasing to the public heart. The doctrine of God's absolute sovereignty is just as true as it was in the days of King Œdipus or of Calvin. It will always remain a confessed fact, that God's will must be the supreme will of the world, but while this is confessed, yet we do perceive that our age as a fact, passes over the great absolutism in silence, compared with the age of Athens or Geneva, and God's love and sweet Fatherhood become more visible than His absolute despotism.

To pass by a truth, is not to contradict it, nor despise it, any more than to study the law is to despise or deny the claim of science or theology. To pass by a truth is often nothing else than to sail by England when your destiny is France, or to omit France when your errand is to England. It is not a condemnation, but a selection. It is not possible that any one age shall make use of all known truths at once and equally, for truth is like a grand armory where are stored all the equipments for warfare, but from which it is not to be expected that every arm and flag and chariot and signal shall be withdrawn at any one time. The armory is a place to draw from, but not to exhaust.

The world of truth is always greater than the world of men, and hence there will always be great truths lying in silence and in neglect, like fields in fallow waiting for some future season that shall demand them for a new sowing and harvest.

In the realm of principles, as in the old world of the classics, there are great silences and solitudes. In our American continent there are vast countries from which man in his civilized state long since departed, leaving behind him ruins of former magnificence, now overgrown with the ivy and the cactus. The vales are richer than New England, and the climate fairer than that which roars about these lakes, but yet man has gone away, leaving traces of his heart and mind in the carved rocks, and terraced gardens. Thus society marches away from one part of the dominion of truth, and, dying, leaves its children to roam to some other shore, perhaps more bleak, perhaps more like to paradise. When one generation passeth away, it will nearly always be found that it took a great deal with it, movable property, gifts, relics, household gods. And when the other generation cometh, lo! in its arms are strange new things, very sacred, and the centres of new hopes and action. Fugitives from famine or fire, try to carry with them household divinities. Exiled generations going from life, have their arms full of customs and ideas that never are seen again on our shores — customs which they could assimilate into healthy food for the soul, but which were rejected by their children.

Next to the supersedure of truths, comes the expansion or contraction of ideas that remain. About many moral statements there hangs always an indefiniteness that makes it possible for each era to expand or contract them. Physical truths may be retained in one form. At our national Capitol there are standards of the inch, the bushel, the quart, the pound, so that the silk or grain of this year may be bought and sold by the measurement agreed upon in the past. It is said that the old kings of Egypt became so anxious that measurements in that kingdom, should forever remain the same, that they built the pyramids, that upon their immovable sides, and in their minute recesses, the empire might always find the standard of all surveys and measurements, from the miles of the highway, to the smallest measure of wheat and wine. When we come to moral ideas, however, we are compelled to do without any standards. There is no stone pyramid to which we can go to adjust our line, no hollowed rock in which we can pour our quart of wine to see if it corresponds to the quart of the Egyptian kings of four thousand years ago. There are thousands of people who will not confess this to be true, and who will contend that they do possess a stone pyramid upon whose sides they can measure all the ideas of religion and duty, but after years of careful search, you will find yourself unable to discover their pyramid in the objective world. It is only a mental structure, a life-long hallucination.

To illustrate this part of our discourse, let us take the idea of "Church." Let the Episcopalians define it, and certain demands are essential that are rejected by the Presbyterians. Let the Presbyterian define it, and he has come into conflict with the Baptist and the Covenanter. Along come the Plymouth Brethren and define the Church to be a body of men assembling, for the hour, to worship. They may never assemble again, but while they were together they were a Church. Dr. Hodge, the most learned thinker the Presbyterians have in this age, declares the Church to be in the heart, and that each soul that loves Christ, is a member of the Church.

Now this is what I mean by the elasticity of a moral idea. These notions are enlarged or contracted, according to the genius of the generation that comes to them here or there. All moral ideas, from the conception of God, to the most humble duty, all doctrines from faith, hope and charity, to the notion of heaven and hell, suffer or undergo this sliding form of measurement, and baffle all attempts to render a final and exact expression. They are infinite in the mathematical sense of the term.

Having now seen that ideas are wont, in some instances, to withdraw from the human arena, and in other instances to undergo limitation or expansion, let us inquire what influence we should expect our land to exert upon the Christian ideas that have invaded it from foreign shores. That no changes would be wrought, could be believed only by those who suppose themselves to possess the standards of measurement, to own a pyramid of solid rock. This is a small multitude, indeed not a multitude at all, but a group. That no changes would be wrought might be the opinion of persons giving no thought to the matter. Of these, the multitude is large indeed. That changes, many and valuable, should be expected, is certainly the conclusion of all who, with free minds, pay any attention to the common influence of government and climate and race over the thoughts of mankind. Just what and how many these changes are, time would fail us here to inquire. You may at your leisure carry forward the task we begin, and you will find the whole matter to a high degree, pleasing and useful.

Coming to a land of gigantic human industry, where the motto is, each one is the builder of his own fortune, to a land where a farmer boy in Kentucky bears himself forward to the place of chief orator, or where a penniless youth lifts himself up to be a millionaire, and a noble citizen; and where this is occurring all the time, the daily phenomenon of the last fifty years, Christianity must expect its fatalism to be shaded, and its doctrine of human freedom and responsibility to stand forth in a more brilliant light. The surrender of all things to God, the resolution of life into a waiting for fate, or into a machine that was powerless to go or to stop of itself, was a conception of God suited to an age when citizens possessed no liberty as to their state, and no industry as to changing their fortune or fame or happiness. An idle country, and an oppressed, powerless country, always underrate the human will, and overstate the Divine interference. Having been denied the privilege and opportunity of toiling for self, men have at last resolved self into despair, and God into an absolute despot.

A free country where the human will and personality rise up into such grand proportions, is the land that might be expected to transform man into a being of personal power, and God into a Father, acting in harmony with His children. The monks in their cells, the middle ages in their bondage to kings, priests and ignorance, possessed no great consciousness of free agency, and hence that was the generation to ignore man, and to enthrone a pitiless fate under the name of God; but the age which, in a perfectly free country, permits every man to carve out for himself a happiness, and education, and fame, is the age to develop the consciousness of free agency, and hence the age to bind more nearly together, man and God, as acting in concert. Political freedom develops the human consciousness of free will and responsibility.

This perpetual industry amid external pursuits, also diverts the mind from the study of mysteries, to the acceptance and enjoyment of facts, and hence the public mind turns away from predestination and reprobation and absolutism, not simply because it has developed a consciousness of freedom, but also because in the long association with facts, it has lost love for the study of the incomprehensible, in both religion and philosophy. In this casting off of old garments, it no more cheerfully throws away the inconceivable of Christianity, than tne inconceivable of Kant and Spinoza. In this abandonment,there is no charge of falsehood cast upon the old mysteries; they may or may not be true; there is only a passing them by as not being in the line of the current wish or taste, raiment for a past age, perhaps for a future, but not acceptable in the present.

Out of this enlargement of the office of man's free will, have come the great missionary movements, and the Sunday and ragged schools of our land. The philosophy of waiting for God has been quite superseded by the enormous development of industry and free-agency that our land has produced. Man is raised, not to a state of vanity, but of responsibility. He feels that God waits for His children to come to His help against the mighty. Here and there a fatalist remains to remind us of the stupor and palsy of antiquity. A Cincinnati clergyman has recently published a labored article to show that Christianity is spreading as rapidly as God desires, and that all human efforts to hasten the world's evangelization are vain and presumptuous; but this ignoring of man's office as a co-laborer of God on earth, this assumption of man's living death is a phenomenon appearing but rarely on the horizon of our republic. Types of men, like types of birds or beasts, pass away slowly, as sometimes an individual creature is found after science has declared the species to have become entirely extinct. Thus types of belief die slowly.

That God has assigned man a work to do here in this vale, and that He has equipped man for doing it, is an idea cast forward greatly by a republic full of human freedom and human achievements. A religion of repose is killed by a politics of activity.

Permit me, therefore, to assume that our republic has tended toward the overthrow of the ideas of human insignificance and of fatality, and of simple divine despotism; and, transforming God into a Father, has made man a co-laborer without whose assistance the moral world pauses just as the plow stands still when man deserts the field for a life of indolence. Man's relations to morals and to agriculture are the same so far as human vision can scan the landscape.

Passing by this illustration of the influence of our land upon religious ideas we may find another example in the distinction now made between doctrines, a discrimination that divides them rapidly in essential and non-essential ideas. In the past, not remote, not only was there a vast multitude of dogmas but they were all deemed very vital. To hold to apostolic succession or to immersion, or to psalmody, or to infant baptism, or to the divineness of slavery was deemed a large part of soul salvation. A free soil politician was an infidel, and on the opposite, a slave-holder had a poor prospect ot heaven. Here we need not particularize. You all know by heart all this black page in church history.

Well, along came a country in which everything was destined to be vast. It embraced every climate, every wood, every ore, every grain,and fruit. Its waters assumed every shape from ocean to lake, from mighty river to mountain brook. Its railways were to run three thousand miles in a straight line, and, starting among New England pines, to end among Pacific orange groves. All nations were to meet in the citizens of this new world. Over this land so vast there was to float a banner of freedom and equality, education and industry. Such was to be the character of the new realm except that words are not able to paint the image in the prophecy. In the gradual fulfillment of this prophesy, which has already gone beyond the promise, it readily came to pass that all that is small in religion began to become manifest as such. The daily struggle amid great things, with the heart full of only leading ideas, built up early a special sense that could discern the large and the small in wealth, in machinery, in agriculture, in character and in Christianity. Ideas that had once been immense underwent great reduction in this uprising of thought, and ideas in themselves infinite, such as Christ, and worship, and faith, charity, virtue, these, vast as the oceans around and the continent between them, came at once into power, not by accident, but by the command of a land of vast spirit and destiny. The whole drift of the country was toward a sifting of thoughts.

Not only did the vastness of the land toil toward this result, but the internal genius of it by which a hundred nations were contributing different races and tongues to be moulded into one brotherhood, made it essential that ideas in which the multitudes differed should be speedily forgotten, and that those in which they agreed only should be remembered and cherished.

Now, the essential ideas of morals and salvation, are the ones in which only most minds agree, and hence the nature of the case united with the vast spirit of the country in exalting the great truths of Christianity and in lulling to sleep the infantine dogmas. These are not condemned as wholly useless, much less as false, but are passed by as if in a sweet sleep, which it were cruelty to disturb.

There are truths in Christianity of infinite worth. Without them, the soul is lost. With them it passes along the paths of usefulness here, and comes beyond to paradise. It ought to have been anticipated that a land like this, trained in an air of greatness, and seeking also a brotherhood that would bind many minds in its silken links, would find the absolute essentials in Christian doctrine and give them its hand and heart. It has done so beyond anticipation, and in its arms, loving and omnipotent, it is bearing us along, compelling us to accept of her destiny as our own. It is vain we were taught the Calvinistic creed, for we perceive the Arminian is borne along equally toward heaven. It is vain we were taught the Arminian creed, for we perceive the Calvinist is just as far toward God's love and bliss. O beautiful disregard of names! The country in declaring all men to be one, and in its greatness and in its effort to make a brotherhood in society, has invaded the domain of the spirit, and, plucking our badges from our bosom, has whispered, "You are all one brotherhood, also in religion." Thus have we built up a state whose soul has outgrown the body politic and has marched into the temple of God. We remember now the German cottager's dream. His humble cot, while he slept, lifted up its rafters and became a cathedral. The chimney became a spire. The windows became gothic and filled with colored glass. His fireplace became an altar, and his children, living and gone, became seraphim bending over that mercy-seat.

Thus while you and I sleep our state becomes a sanctuary. Its liberty, its free will, its greatness of idea, its equality of man, its brotherhood, all enter our once humble abode and lift it all upward and outward as in the transformation of that German dream.

It is impossible for the state to be engaged making us brothers and the church to be engaged making us enemies and strangers. One or the other effort must abandon the field. The church bows justly to the spirit of the republic. In India, two communion tables are spread so that the converted Brahmin may not touch the cup the poor native of low caste has polluted. This is an easy result in India, but where the state makes all one, then religion also hastens to accept of the harmony.

You may, my friends, at your leisure, seek and find further instances of this modification of Christian belief by the new surroundings of government. Christian customs will also be modified along with the creed. Not that something absolutely better will always be found, but something more demanded by the accidents of the time. The themes of the pulpit will always be assigned afresh by each new generation. When our catechisms were being written, the chief enemy upon the horizon was the Romanist full of error and cruelty, and hence many are the darts aimed by the Westminster soldiers at the papal hosts. With the overthrow of the papal throne new arrows and armor are demanded for new foes. The field of battle shifts from Paul to Genesis. The thumb-screw of the inquisition is not so much feared as the spade of the geologist. The mass and prayers for the dead are not so alarming as the crucible of the chemist. It is not Arius and Arminius now that we fear. It is Darwin and Buckle. New methods also arise. Once it was enough if the pulpit brought out to the multitude the statements found in the Holy Scriptures, but now the public has learned what is in the Scriptures, they ask us to prove that the Scriptures are holy. To unfold the text was the easy task of our fathers; to find the warrant of the text is the more difficult work of their children. A new method divested of authority and weighed down with rationalism and doubt, has gradually displaced the authoritative declaration and warning of yesterday. Christ comes not announced by a simple herald, but led by a spiritual and intellectual philosophy. The soul is asked to receive its own in the name of virtue, pardon and future life. The banner of the cross is borne by the impulse of its own fitness and beauty, rather than by the command of Buller and Paley. When Tyndall flies to the light and heat and dust, Christianity flies to the soul. Thus you will find that the public education has awakened a broader inquiry into branches of learning connected in some way with theology, and hence the pulpit is compelled to discuss themes that were foreign to its office a few years since. With the growth of rationalism, it must more carefully separate the true from the false to meet the new love of the real truth and the new ridicule of all superstition and folly. The truth will no longer bear a great admixture of falsehood.

In this republic of equality that places the rich and poor, the laborer and the clergyman, upon one plane, the whole language of abuse and denunciation has been banished from the sacred desk, so that Thomas Paine, if now alive, would enjoy the undreamed of pleasure of hearing his objections met by hearts of sympathy and tenderness, rather than by the hisses of an age full, equally, of vanity and revenge. Compared with former generations this one, most of all, discards the power of personal egotism based upon peculiar training in peculiar lines of thought, and, offering the right hand, says with a friendship that would have melted an old infidel to tears, "Come let us reason together."

But time fails me. There are some general statements I desire yet to make.

There need be no alarm about this abrasion of an old shore by a new wave, for we know that what the waters are stealing from some old bank where men have ceased to live, they are depositing elsewhere and making new homes for a better race, new streets for greater cities. The wave that carries something away always gives something back elsewhere to mankind. The coast changes, not the sea. And furthermore the abrasions upon the old shore are limited, for the encroaching sea deals only with alluvium or drift, and, having swept this clean by a hundred years' toil, it finds at last an admantine rock—an iron-bound coast where the waters cease their destruction, and, their work done, praise God in peace or storm.

> "And all through winter's storm and summer's calm,
> They rise and fall an everlasting psalm."

Thus Christianity possesses within itself, in its central Christ and doctrines, a coast, iron-bound, where all waves of thought must pause and become an anthem of divine praise, full of human hope and human gratitude.

In this rise and fall of ideas it is not very wonderful that we perceive no great commotion, and nowhere in orthodox denominations perceive any arraignment of individuals for departures from the faith. This absence of trials for heresy comes, not simply from the fact that there is little heresy in the case, for this has never been an influential fact, but this wide and deep peace comes from two other facts, first, that the age bears all its ministry toward the essential ideas and absorbs them at these points; and, second, that so far as there are any new departures they are universal rather than individual. If they were the new departures of one man there would be trial and discord, but they are the modifications of a whole generation, rather than the light of any individual. Whatever there is of the new in the present it has come to all equally and gently as the dew in the night. The jury is *particeps criminis* in the great case.

So far as my own vision can penetrate, and judgment infer,

the pastors of this city in the denomination to which I belong, are of one mind in theological questions. It may be that some surpass others in admiration of the German maxim that " Silence is golden," and hence, have a better developed virtue of reticence, but to me, in an intimate acquaintance with all, they seem all borne along in the wide arms of a country that has been the instrument under God, of revealing to them all the breadth and kindness of the Christian religion

Generation passeth away, and generation cometh. This means that you will all soon become dust. The great invisible arms that are carrying religion and all ideas along, are carrying your body to its place in the waving grass, and your spirit back to God. Oh my friends, love that religion, that by command of God fits itself so well to our country, our happiness, our life, our death. Say not it was for the past. Its superstition was for that; its truth is for the present and future. It assumes the image of the soul, and hence, was made, not for woman and for childhood, but for the human race. Our state builds up liberty. Christianity absorbs the idea and advances to freedom of the spirit. Our state demands public virtue. Christianity's favorite maxim is, " Blessed are the pure in heart." Our state loves humanity. Christianity silently points to Jesus Christ. Pass it not by. Oh may this generation, while it is passing along, number among its transformations, the transformation of your hearts into the image of the Saviour, that when, after a few years, it shall have strewn all your bodies like autumn leaves upon the earth, it may waft your spirits, redeemed and sanctified, back to your Maker.

THE JOYFUL SUNDAY.*

DAVID SWING.

"For My yoke is easy and My burden is light."—*Matthew xi : 30.*

Three facts combine to place this Sunday beyond the reach of the pulpit's prose. We would do well to surrender the occasion to song, and flowers, and the full heart's meditation. It is a Sunday in springtime; it is a Sunday of the holy communion, and it is Easter Sunday. May your hearts all find in their own depths a measurement of the occasion which words cannot express. What help you may not gather from the pulpit's formal words to-day, you may find in the flowers that wreathe the altar and in the spiritual associations of the hour. What remarks you are invited to hear shall be in some way suggested by the presence and character of the Easter Day.

It is only conjecture that has located this sacred anniversary upon the border of spring. Many of those details which are carefully reported in an age of printing, and in an age of such restless inquiry as the art of printing has developed, wholly escaped record and remembrance in the far-off times of the Testament. The history of modern events is gathered by hundreds of busy hands, and hundreds of presses multiply the exact report, so that the day that witnesses the end of a war, or the death of a great individual, places in the hand of every citizen a history of the great war or the great life. History, worthy in a high sense of the name, begins with the art of printing. All history, up to the coming of that "art preservative of all arts," is only a poor outline of a world, instead of a full-faced picture of the great subject. It is comforting to the Christian, however, to feel that the life of his Master is full beyond the custom of profane biography, and in detail of the life, and thoughts, and deeds, and death, surpasses the chronicles the world possesses as to any great character of the far past, not excepting such a philosopher as Plato, or such an emperor as Cæsar. The life of Christ is remarkable for the number of its witnesses, and for the credibility they merit by their honesty and opportunity. But they gave us no birthday nor deathday of their Master, and after the old, half-civilized generations in the Third century had absolutely fought battles over different

* Sermon delivered in the Fourth Presbyterian Church, April 5, 1874.

opinions about the time of the resurrection, the Council of Nice established a day by decree, and since that date the Christian Church has, so far as it has regarded the event at all, celebrated the morning which our generation is learning to love more and more deeply.

Aside from the exact day, it is quite probable that this event of sorrow and joy occurred in the spring months, for as the Christian Church followed closely with its life the event of the cross, it is hardly probable that the oldest persons in the first century should have possessed incorrect data regarding the season of the year when their Lord was crucified, and that they should have located in the spring an event so significant that occurred in the late harvest or mid-winter. It seems quite certain that the Lord thus died and arose in the spring time, and thus by design, for there is not much of accident in the world, associating His life and His religion with the realm of flowers, and beauty, and hope. Spring is the peculiar property of hope. We all, from the young child to the most venerable father of three score and ten years, feel that when the long winter relents and the wind has begun to blow softly upon the cheek, a new world is about to come, and each morning bird song seems a herald declaring a new joy and new existence to the heart. There are many wonderful harmonies between the God of nature and the God of the soul. They are so numerous that the spirit of man can express all its varying conditions by asking us to look upon the world of material. If unhappy, it declares its sky to be clouded; if happy, its sky to be bright; if young, it appeals to springtime as its emblem; if beyond manhood, and forsaken, it cries,

> "My name is in the yellow leaf,
> The flowers and fruits of love are gone;
> The worm, the canker, and the grief
> Are mine alone."

Thus there are no shadings in human experience which may not behold their image in the great temple of nature in which man lives and dies. The majority of mortals come upon death in the night hours, as though the great evening shadow which wraps in its gloom wood and field, and even the loved home where the sick one lies, were designed of God to be an accompaniment to the shadow about to come to the spirit. If, therefore, the God of nature and the God of the heart are seen to move along in such parallel lines, why may we not suppose that if a Savior was to come and rise from the tomb in presence of a world, that the infinite wisdom would ask the great springtime to open her flower beds for that tomb of new life and hope. It is only one of a thousand harmonies if that season which casts its best sunshine and happiness upon the shores of earth, is that one which was asked to cast the Son of Man upon the shores of immortality.

When the Easter Sunday became established it was called *dominica gaudii*—"the joyful Sunday"—and thus for fifteen hundred years this day has journeyed along to receive not the offerings of dust and ashes, not the worship of sighing and despair, but the offerings of the sweetest bloom and the worship of gratitude and hope. A large part of the Protestant world has faithfully closed its eyes to the reality and value of this anniversary in Christian history, and thus has robbed religion of one of its beautiful robes, leaving it more and more dependent upon a costume of nothing but sackcloth. The reason of this past neglect is manifold. Protestantism in its puritan and dissenting divisions was a reaction against a service of an extremely material character. The spiritual seemed forgotten, and the outward symbols to have taken the place of an "inner life." The pulpit that had been set up in early years as a teacher of truth, had been crowded almost out of existence by a great stage filled with bishops, priests, and acolytes, where eloquence seemed deposed by pageantry. Against a religion which seemed an extravagant development of the spectacular, Presbyterianism, and Methodism, and Congregationalism, and Quakerism, were a form of revolt, for it cannot be denied that the creed of these new sects was not such a full departure from Episcopacy or Romanism as was the genius of their new worship, its spirituality and simplicity. Having set forth in a full dislike of the state Churches, and particularly of the Roman Church, these independent sects feared and despised everything Roman, and hence saw the hand of Satan not only in the "confessional," and in the "infallibility," but also in a Church organ and in Easter happiness.

A second reason for this neglect may be found in the fact that these dissenting sects arose further north than Palestine, and Italy, and France, and amid hardships of government, of sky, of race, and hence amid severity of thought; hence religion omitted much that was beautiful and gentle, and dealt greatly in the logical and the most practical; and if any further reflection is needed to account for the neglect which this day receives in many puritan branches of the church, we may remember that the Free sects have been compelled to fight their whole way along through history, and hence could not accomplish much with a sword in one hand and Easter flowers in the other. The poetry of religion died in the long conflict.

In the joy and gratitude of this day our hearts should not fail to be thankful that the world has so advanced in the enlightenment which destroys prejudice, and in the deeper study of religion, and in the development of a Christian brotherhood, that now at last this day comes back to our sanctuary and excites no ill will, no past bitter memory of pope or bishop, but only remembrances of the open tomb of Arimathea. The Christian heart universal is so emptied of old animosity and narrowness that the Protestant Churches rejoice, I believe, to join this day with the Catholic world in confessing the religious worth and beauty of this occasion, and in joining with them, though at separate altars, in this worship of joyfulness.

In coming up to such a day as this, we have not encountered a kind of accident of the religion of Jesus, but have come to its inmost and permanent spirit. When the Divine Author of religion declares that " His yoke is easy and His burden light," we may accept of the words as covering all the days of this pilgrimage. When looked at from the standpoint of old Jewish law, full of imperfections, full of wrath, and too narrow either for life or death, whose confines were a single nation, and whose religion was an external offering of flocks, and whose great emblem was a Sinai covered with thunderings and vivid lightnings, Christ's yoke, with its perfection of reason in its new law, and with its redemption on the cross, and with its forgiveness, and its brotherhood of man and loving presence of God, became easy and His burden light.

When the Testament in many places assures us that whoever would follow Christ must deny himself and take up the cross, it would seem that Christianity was sent forth on a mission of sorrow; but much of that language was directed to those immediate times when to follow Christ was to place the foot in a path which led to martyrdom. It was necessary for a St. Paul and for tens of thousands around his grave to turn away from the paths of earthly happiness, and bidding farewell to friends, to look death calmly in the face as the fate of the morrow not far away. The prayer of Milton over the martyrs of Piedmont passes beyond his horizon and becomes full of awful solemnity when breathed over the first four centuries after our Lord:

> "Forget not: in Thy book record their groans
> Who were Thy sheep, and in their ancient fold
> Slain by the bloody Piedmontese that rolled
> Mother with infant down the rocks. Their moans
> The vales redoubled to the hills and they to heaven,
> Their martyr'd blood and ashes sow
> O'er all the Italian fields."

In view of these dark ages, whose fury it seems was not wholly to die away for a thousand years, Christ handed down to His children the form of His own cross to go with them, the emblem of many a sorrow and many a martyrdom. Thus I feel that many of the half-melancholy words of Christ were spoken as against the persecutions that would follow and did exhaust themselves upon that special shore, leaving His broadest and everlasting declaration to be that of our text: "My yoke is easy and My burden is light." Sorrows may come here and there, to this or that period, or to this or that heart, but as a general truth embracing all lands and all humanity, Christianity is the most abundant fountain of happiness of whose waters the human family may ever drink. If there is any happiness in this world it ought to be found in the obedience of such morals as are found in the Sermon upon the Mount, and in such a life of broad love and charitable action as are seen in the life of Christ, and in that refuge for the soul found beneath His Cross, and in that hope which there bursts upon the vision beyond the open tomb.

If I should declare that apart from the fear of persecution and martyrdom there is no cross to be borne, I should overlook a certain self-denial which does indeed belong to this religion. But it is almost worthy of contempt, for it is not a denial of a *good self* but of a *wicked self*. We are not asked to deny self of anything that belongs to the broadest and highest development of mind and heart, but if there is anything low and satanic in our nature, we are invited to cut off that form of human energy. Self-denial seems to be a denying the heart the privilege of its own self-disgrace. If not to steal, not to envy, not to bear false witness, not to despise the poor, nor be insensible to the wants of one's fellow-men, are a self-denial, then Christianity is full of it; but if we pass by a depraved or unworthy nature as being something whose gratifications is a simple disgrace, and if we think of only a lofty soul and the highest form of character, Christianity is not a self-denial, but a self-love and self-gratification. Much of the asceticism which lingers in the Christian philosophy and practice has been gathered up from half-civilized ages, all through which religion advanced mingled with the horrid ideas of paganism. As the Hindoos try to please their gods by hook-swinging and by thrusting hot irons through the flesh, so the semi-Christian times, lingering on the borders of this pagan darkness, have had their saints of pillar and cave; and as the children of Bengal have for thousands of years run forth to see the fakirs coming into the village, cutting their own bodies with knives, so have the Christian villagers in Europe followed in wonder and reverence a procession of flagelants marching to a chorus of whips, and with feet sprinkled with blood. Both these scenes, one in India under Vishnu, the other in Europe under Christ, are pictures of the same human heart living in a native ignorance which was still bringing to bear upon the new Gospel a folly of logic and of soul that had long been producing the deformities of religion along the Tiber and Nile and Ganges. Wherever a Christian has starved himself, wherever a Christian has worn a girdle of thorns, wherever a Christian mother has tried to love her children less, that she might love her God more, wherever a saint has withdrawn from the bright sunlight that he might dwell only in the light of God, wherever any heart anywhere has felt that by self-imposed suffering it might gratify God the more, there all these well-meaning ones have revealed not the import of Christianity, but the dark shadow of that realm beyond Christ, where the mother drowns her infant for God's sake, and where strong men have in the name of God held up their right arm till it withered, or have gazed at the sun till they became blind forever. Many an age has groaned under what they called the "Cross," which instead of being a cross was only a *folly*. When Mme. Guyon resolved that she would not feel sad when her children should die, but would lay them in the grave as she had put them in the cradle at night, and when we perceive that this she actually did, and shed no tear, but smiled on them dead as she had smiled on them living, we must not be betrayed even by her rank and culture or fortune into the belief that she was unveiling any of the mysteries of our religion, but must confess that her great mind and heart were touched by that shadow of infirmity which has thrown its dark line in some form across all the intellects which have ever lived, however great or humble. Every soul born into the world is born into mistakes. Be the intellect lofty as that of a Demosthenes or a Matthew Hale, be the genius as divine as that of Dante or Shakespeare, be the heart as sweet as that of Fenelon or Cowper, across it somewhere will fall a dark line, the shadow of man's frailty, reminding us that there is none good but God. Escaping from this influence of innate infirmity and of surrounding barbarism, and coming up face to face before the actual religion of Christ, we are bound to confess that its yoke is easy and its burden light. The escape from a low life to a higher one, the refuge from sin found in the Rifted Rock and in forgiveness, the new love toward all mankind and toward God, the better reading of life's significance, and the perpetual looking to heaven from amid all the sorrows of this shore, should not be confessed a cross for bowed-down shoulders, but rather a joyful crown for the temples.

There is one consideration which tends to rob Christianity of that lightness of heart which belongs to the innocence of childhood and to the absolute pleasure-seekers of mature years. It has not so loud a laugh, nor so many sunshiny days. But the reason of this is so vast and so noble that one might well accept of its sacrifice of merriment, to gain instead the soberness that comes from so honorable a cause. Let the human mind and heart espouse any truth that leads to a deeper study of man, a philosophy that studies the wants of the human family in all its races and ages and conditions, a philosophy which must go along with all these years, and then look over into eternity, a philosophy issuing from an Infinite sympathy and which must go where the orphan is weeping and the sick dying, and this philosophy will be one which, in what we call merriment, can be surpassed always by the childhood which knows nothing, or by the empty years of sin and fashion which nothing cares. As the statesmen who, like Cobden, or Bright, or Lincoln, espouse the destinies of the multitude, are borne away from the butterfly joy which they knew in childhood, and which they can still behold along the fashionable avenues, so Christianity, fully accepted by the soul, brings with it often a study of mankind and a longing for the world's welfare which sobers the waking hours and even invades with its anxiety the once peaceful and sweet world of dream.

Compared, however, with a childish life or a sinful life or an empty life, Christianity is not in our century, escaped as it has from much pagan abnegation, and centering as it does upon an era of love and happiness, any longer a bondage, but its yoke is easy and its burden light. Its cross was borne by its Christ that it might not be borne by His children. The cross weighed down His body and spirit to the tomb, but to His children it is worn on the bosom, an ornament of beauty and hope. Once stained with blood, it is now wreathed with flowers.

Two Sundays in the year are now dedicated to the spirit of happiness. The Protestant Church has now for the most part admitted these two oases into a broad desert, and all that remains is for us to read the Gospel of our Lord that we shall seek to make these two "Sundays of joy," these islands in the sandy plain widen out till the vision of waving palm trees shall always lie before every traveler in this lonely march. When modern art and modern ambition had traced a canal from the Nile to the Suez station, verdure followed the waters through the desert, and now trees wave in blessing where for ages the burning sand blistered the foot and filled the traveler's heart with only a sense of desolation. It is coming to pass, and it will come to be confessed more fully in future times, that Christianity is a stream flowing through a desert world, only that more palm trees may rise up and flowers bloom for the joy of the multitude that move to and fro in these wide plains of life.

Such are our thoughts for the day when the cross of death is wreathed with the flowers of eternal life. In presence of this wreath all others of earth fade. The bride wreathes her forehead in the name of a long friendship, but her beauty and joy, her home, would all become dust after a few years, as perishable as the wreath of her forehead, were it not for the hope of immortal life which wafts her and all she loves forward to a world of unending bliss. So the wreathes of statesmen and philanthropists, of all love and friendship, look to the great resurrection beyond these narrow confines as fulfillment of their hopes and reward of their toils. Hence we have come to-day to the wreath of all wreathes, to the bloom that causes all blossoming. Oh, blessed Easter flowers! the scattered roses of every field cast their color and perfume down before your more sacred import. As the sheaves of his brethren all bowed before the sheaf of Joseph, in the old, beautiful dream, because they saw that his hands would feed the hungry in far-off years, when their own grains had perished, so before the Easter immortelles all the lilies and roses of a wide world may come to worship, because, gifted with prophecy, they may well see in these emblems of immortality a beauty which shall reappear in eternity long after their own leaves shall have been scattered and their perfume all breathed away into the silent night.

SOUL-CULTURE.*

DAVID SWING.

For what is a man profited if he shall gain the whole world and lose his own soul?—*Matt.* xvi. 26. And the Child grew and waxed strong in spirit.—*Luke* ii. 40.

The words soul and spirit are sprinkled over the pages of the Bible as thickly as leaves upon the ground in autumn. There is no evident difference in the signification of the two words. A book has been published within the past two years, whose object is to teach that man is composed of three elements—mind, soul, and spirit; but most readers rise from the book entertained to some extent, but to a greater extent untaught and bewildered.

Beyond the grand divisions, mind and soul, it is difficult to pass. And these two continents are not marked out by definite coast lines and separated by great neutral oceans, but rather lie contiguous, like the two tints of a flower, with a beautiful middle ground, where the spectator loses power to announce which color is more vivid.

But for our purpose we do not need a definite mapping out of mind and soul, intellect and spirit, knowledge and character; we need only the general truth, that man possesses a certain soul-life, that can grow and can rise and fall like the waves of the deep.

It is wonderful how much the Bible uses this word spirit. If you will open your Concordance and see what an array of texts there are in which this word is master of the proposition, you will ever after think more highly of the soul within your own bosom. You will there see set in order the "spirit" of wisdom, the "spirit" of love, the "spirit" of charity, of peace, the "spirit" of God, the broken "spirit," the faithful "spirit," and, according to Peter, the glorious "spirit." Reading over this grand catalogue, made up out of all the deepest thought of Job and St. John, you cannot but feel thankful that the Creator has poured into your bosom a portion of that soul without which the whole world would profit nothing.

I have read these texts not for the purpose of leading you

* A discourse delivered March, 1872, at Standard Hall, by Prof. David Swing, pastor of the Fourth Presbyterian Church.

again over the estimate of that deliverance of spirit announced by Christ, but for the purpose of uttering some thoughts that ought to be held as preliminary to all consideration of that blessed redemption revealed in the New Testament. If there is offered the world a Saviour of the soul, the world may well inquire what the soul is, and whether it is desirable that it struggle much, or long, for a friendship with that great Soul of Nazareth. Our inquiry is not a direct application of the text, but a preliminary reflection.

If one might dare find a defect in the method of preaching the gospel, it would seem safe to declare that the method is one of endless assumption of preliminary thoughts, and endless repetition of final truths and conventional terms. In place of any discussion of the nature of sin, we are warned simply as sinners, and the punishment is daily re-announced. The nature of faith is passed by in our zeal to urge men to believe; the philosophy and analysis of repentance are crowded out of the world by the perennial command to repent; and instead of defining or measuring the inspiration of the sacred Book, it is enough if we say daily that all Scripture is given by inspiration.

Whether this avoidance of preliminary questions is to be attributed to a want of courage, or want of industry, or to a long prevalence of dogmatism which is too vain to admit the importance of an inquiry, we cannot venture to affirm, but must content ourself with the conviction that there is need of reform in the topics and mode of the sacred desk. When, however, we all remember with what labor, and with disappointment often, men have sought the foundation truths of life, we cannot but palliate the sin that gives up this path of pursuit, and accepts of a final word and no questions asked.

All thoughts about the soul must indeed lead us to a wall at last, which we cannot undermine or scale; but such is the common destiny of truth-seekers that our tears of sorrow will fall no sooner here, and no bitterer, than along any path our foot may choose. It is said that Aristotle grieved all his life that he could not explain the tides of the sea that washed the shores of his country. The pursuit of knowledge, like the pursuit of any pleasure, is a chase of both joy and grief. All the nets that drag through the sea of life draw out the good and bad at last to the shore. All the seventy years are a constant effort to sift the varied sorrow out of those seventy years; and when at last we fall, the winnowing fan will be found in the right hand, trying still to separate grain and chaff. But, unreadable as all things are in the world, there are always approximations to truth possible on all hands, and with these our hearts must learn to be content.

In this matter of intellect and soul, it is not otherwise.

Though there are places where colors blind and are lost, or where light ends in shadow, yet there is some color and some light. I am inclined to think that the soul is the conscious life or being of man, and that intellect is simply its grandest servant, its daily purveyor. A new fact is valuable because it feeds this inner life. It helps the soul to some new motion or deed of joy. Knowledge is fuel for this warm flame. The Psalmist says that while he was musing the fire burned—not the fire upon the hearth—but the flame in his bosom. He says, "My heart was hot within me," and while he mused the fire burned the more intensely. That is, as the facts passed along in review before his intellect, his soul within him increased the flow and power of its life.

Knowledge is said to be power. It is indeed power, for the soul converts it into all manner of action—joy, charity, worship, love, eloquence. As the rich earth drinks in simply water and light and heat, and then sends forth all manner of fruit and blossoms, so the soul receives the facts of the intellect, and makes them the basis of a vast creation, varied as that which came from the Almighty.

To the poor negro, lying on the banks of the Niger, what a narrowness of soul! What a perpetual stupor! But how could his soul live or move? The facts of the world have never fallen upon it, as dew upon drooping grass. The vast culture of the world, the vast arts useful and beautiful, its immense history, running back through thousands of years and over vast empires, have never passed into his brain, and the soul, having no purveyor, starves within its silent dungeon. The spirit of this poor savage is a seed that has fallen upon a rock. There is nothing to nourish its mysterious germ. Tendrils thrown out could grasp nothing; hence there is no unfolding of leaf or flower.

Compare with this desolate soul a Burke that was cast among the facts of England, or a disciple that leaned upon the heart of the world's Lord, and saw truths turning into soul. The facts of earth are only the food ordained of Heaven for the life of the spirit. Besides the common five senses, there is an innumerable army of purveyors—history, science, art, religion—whose only calling is that of adding to the emotions and impulses of that mystery called soul. The truths of this whole career are only the soil of that strange but beautiful growth, the spirit.

Truth, therefore, sought through simple desire to increase one's store of acquisition, truth pursued only to learn what comes next, must be much like the miser's pursuit of gold—a fatal transformation of a means into an end. As money is worthless, only so far as the blessings of life are bought with it, so the acquisition of knowledge must have its value measured by the outgrowth of sentiment.

The decoration and enlargement of the heart are the direct end of truth, and, without this result, knowledge is not power, but is treasure buried and forgotten—like the fabled gold of Capt. Kidd—by some unknown sea. Florence Nightingale is all the prison truth and battle-field truth of the world turned into divine soul. Those gloomy facts were converted into an infinite love by the strange machinery of man.

A Christian's creed, therefore, is only a first step toward being a Christian or even a good man. He has facts, just as a successful speculator has money, but whether the man will be a Christian is as uncertain as whether the gainer of money will be a noble man or a despicable miser. It is the fire which truth kindles in the soul that determines the value of all study and experience and reflection. Hence the grand men of the world have never been those who have acquired most truths, but those with whom the world's experience and events have hastened to put on the garments of divine spirit, those with whom truth has been only a hand to strike afresh each day the spirit's harp. Hence it has easily come to pass that the most useless and forlorn men who have lived since the world began have been the professional heresy-hunters in the Church. Living for a certain assemblage of words just as the miser lives for his labeled bags of gold, they have always left their souls to go dressed in vile rags and to die of famine in absolute sight of a land of milk and honey. Not knowing "that an ounce of life is better than a ton of knowledge," they are but clerks who file the business transactions of yesterday and await calmly the arrival of some morrow of dispute. These having read a page, or having had an opportunity of hearing a discourse, do not open their souls to admit any new warmth, but with Shylock begin to read the record, and to mutter that "it is not so stated in the bond." The idea of character never disturbs their brain, but man's prospect of heaven is learned wholly by a comparison of antique bonds. Instead of seeking the grandeur of man in the soul's alembic, where truth is passing over into the realm of spirit, they locate salvation in their forty articles, and give to prejudice and to memory the heavens that God made for the heart. These have never been the useful or loved men of history. They are the misers of Christianity. But when there has come along a being with whom a single fact in morals has fallen in upon that holy place called the soul, and burst forth into some sweet sentiment, there has come along a being that was both earth's help and earth's joy.

In Wilberforce, the fact of negro bondage fell in upon his heart like a flower seed falling into the warm black earth of Italy or

Florida. His one truth produced a tear. His tear increased into a river of eloquence. The river widened into the modern Sea of Liberty. His soul absorbed that truth of suffering and became all colored with a Christ-like humanity, as the snow white wool drinks in the Tyrian dye. Alongside this Wilberforce place a score of professional heresy-hunters fresh from their victim, and how wretched they all appear in presence of such an uprising of a single heart!

There is no doubt the notorious Catherine II. held more truth and better truth than was known to all classic Greece—held to a belief in a Saviour, of whose glory that gifted land knew nought; and yet, such is the grandeur of soul above mind, that I doubt not that Queen Penelope of the dark land, and the doubting Socrates, have found at Heaven's gate a sweeter welcome sung of angels than greeted the ear of Russia's brilliant, but false-lived queen. Penelope knew little about our God, nothing about our Saviour; but what truth she knew was transfigured in the white raiment of life—the garb of immortality.

"Virtue is knowledge applied," says a thoughtful writer. And Cicero says: "Why should I study unless to prepare myself for my associations with my fellow men?" Beautiful thought of that unrivaled man! Why read the history of liberty unless I intend to grasp it with a firmer hand, and seek to break the chains of humanity? Why study the flowers of the field unless I am to come home tenderer to my children, and a better believer in God? Why read over the world's charity unless I am myself henceforth to be of kinder heart?

Thus the Christian creed is valuable only so far as the soul can and does draw it into its crucible and transform it into life. The variations between Methodist and Calvinist go for nought, because the variations are over ideas that are incapable of being made into the fibre of soul. They count nothing because they do not reach the realm where God stretches at last the line of measurement.

It is not the Trinity that moulds human life, but the doctrine of God. It is not the eternal possession of the Holy Spirit that may shape the human soul, but the fact of an ever-present spirit. That Christ was eternally begotten of the Father is a doctrine that cannot be appreciated in any way by man's heart, but the Christ of the New Testament can be grasped and loved; and hence the responsibility and success and beauty of human life will be all related to the latter of these statements, and be wholly discharged from all the former, without penalty or costs.

That truth alone is valuable and filled with responsibility, which might make our life deeper and better. To slight this is to lose that soul, than which one would better lose the whole world. Those are the responsible facts which lie above our hearts as the pure snow on the mountains lies ready to bless in summer time the fields beneath.

Intellect is said to be cold. So it is by itself. But complain not at the snow that reposes upon the Rocky or Alpine range. Cold? Yes. But all summer long, and long is the summer at their bases, the vineyards and fields and orchards draw their clusters, their golden harvests, from the kind melting of these treasures of the frost. Cold, indeed, but all of France and Italy are made a paradise beneath.

Truth in itself is cold, but in the design of the Creator its white treasures falling as softly as snow, and falling through many centuries, daily dissolve and transform the spirit beneath into a never-fading paradise.

Our material earth is built by many layers wrapped around it in its long history. Geologists dig to great depths or go where the earthquake has made openings miles in depth, and lo! the lowest ground or rock is found to have been formed by the falling of leaves and grasses, and by the varied wrappings of the ages gone. It is now known that the atmosphere is raining forever an invisible dust upon this ball, making it larger and warmer and more beautiful. The rock scraped by a glacier becomes covered, and invites moss and lichen to its breast.

The human soul is such a world. The truths of to-day, of yesterday, of the whole past are settling down upon it a golden rain from the hand of God, making the glorious wrappings of time and of the great futurity. Thus the dark facts of earth, its slavery, its suffering, its sickness, its calamities, its burned up cities, its solemn cemeteries of the dead, all may be transformed into human spirit and make the soul come to heaven at last rich in its tenderness and love. The earthly knowledge is made into never dying power. Bulwer says, "Oh how much greater is the soul of one man than the vicissitudes of the whole globe!" And elsewhere he says, "Not in the knowledge of things without, but in the perfection of the soul within, lies the true empire of man."

From considerations such as these, I am inclined to think that mystery is also a servant of the soul trying to give it some shade of beauty which no plain fact could even paint upon it. To eliminate vanity, to overthrow egotism, to check the footsteps in the path of sin, to keep the soul tender, to bring the king down to the level of his servant, I can conceive of nothing more powerful than the mystery of death. When the mother thinks of it she bids her children good night with a deeper love and with a more intense prayer that God will be an angel over them by night. By mystery our philosophers are made to be as children, and, indeed, the hearts of all educated beings are lifted up by its sad but strong arms above the dust of earth, and are borne nearer the infinite throne. As though the events of earth were insufficient to exalt us, realms are created where unseen hands smite the heart strings, and where the air trembles with a grand unknown melody.

It is not probable that the Creator has poured out darkness around man only to harrass him on life's march. All things are ordered for good, and it must be that to the facts that educate mankind, mystery adds the shadow of facts, to carry this education along some new paths. When the world sums up educational influences, it enumerates success, and acts, and languages. But this estimate is too rude and coarse, for a human friend, deeply loved and long known, often casts over the soul a culture which all schools would have failed to bestow. Indeed, from the closets of the great schools, we go forth with empty hands, compared with the treasures which we carry from the bosom of the noble mother, where we spent all early years, and from the earth and sky that were the oceans of our island childhood.

Into any survey of educational forces, we must admit, therefore, elements that escape the first rude estimate, and find room for those shadows of awful facts that perpetually hang their dark curtains before us.

As the depth of mystery is only felt by the most civilized and advanced soul, and is a cloud of which a savage knows nothing, it may be inferred, that it comes not as a penalty of culture, but as a delicate hand to lead it to a still better being. The solemn question of Hamlet, "To be, or not to be," surpasses the books of the school-house in shaping the spirit of man. The willow and cypress, that mourn over the tombs of our dead, impress our hearts the more deeply, because the wind that sighs through them, and the somber shades they cast, help us to pass over into the unknown world. Thus, by fact, and by the wandering shadow of fact, the soul of man is perpetually fed. They are the only manna that falls for it, in this wilderness march.

To the natural power of the world's truths it pleased God to add the "truth as it is in Jesus." The soil of earth was too poor to nourish a great soul. Into the common thoughts of society the heavens opened and poured out the vast truths of penitence, faith, charity, purity of heart, and heaven beyond. To live a life amid such surroundings as earth now possesses must be only to live a career of preparation for a world more blessed. To lose one's soul must be to pass through this sublime temple without drinking in its virtue and holy worship, and not only to have rejected the true, but to have suffered the falsehoods of society to rush upon the delicately-strung harp of the spirit, and break its strings, and hush its melodies. "Truth," says the great dramatist, "are the wings wherewith we fly to heaven."

O friends immortal! earth will soon disappear. You will soon pass from its varied scenes. While you walk yet on this mortal land, hold most dear those truths that may be embodied in the heart. Let your creed be measured by the need of your inner life, and let all the duties and joys and grief of life only wrap some more beautiful garment around your spirit. Then, called to go hence, you will bear away with you the good of earth, as the sun, rising from the sea, draws up after him its whitest mist and most delicate colorings.

A MISSIONARY RELIGION.*

DAVID SWING.

Go ye, therefore, and teach all nations.—*Matthew xxviii: 19.*

This being the missionary day of this congregation, it would be a great neglect of duty and of a great theme of inquiry should we simply make an annual offering of gifts. Once a year, at least, we may well look at the cause in its forms of fact and philosophy, and thus enable ourselves to base our contributions upon some knowledge of their destination and value. The Christian religion is nothing but a great mission scheme, of which the world is the field, and Christ the first and the chief of a missionary host. The religious systems up to the Savior's day were systems only for the porch or closet. Most of the moralists were only men of seclusion, men of the grove or the porch, who, pacing to and fro a few steps, spoke as they walked, and thus were dreamers in a secluded spot, rather than messengers to the world. It was necessary for the few who knew of the existence and haunts of these wise men to make long journeys to their presence, and there encamp for a time to drink in the sweet waters of these rare springs. In all those days of Roman and Greek and Indian wisdom, moral systems were a curiosity more than a public cultus, and were studied as a kind of mental exercise, rather than as a mode of daily life.

Whenever a moral system assumed the form of a worship, and attempted to spread itself, as in the Hebrew and Mohammedan states, it spread as a government rather than as a religion. It sought not so much a universal salvation as a universal empire. It will, it seems, be sufficiently true if we affirm that the New Testament religion is the only one that deliberately announced the idea of a world-wide religious crusade, having for its object the spiritual enlightenment and transformation of mankind. It cut religion away from state duties and temptations as from a deadly hindrance, and sent it forth upon a purely spiritual mission. Separating itself from government, the world became its field, and man universal became its object of prayer, and love, and pursuit. Hence Christ used with wonderful significance the word "world." He Himself was the light of the "world," and He sent His disciples into the "world," and the "world" was to be preached to by His messengers, and the end of the

* Sermon delivered in Fourth Presbyterian Church, April 12, 1874.

"world" was to follow this wide evangelization. If you will read carefully the Testament for this purpose, you will perceive that Christianity announced itself not as a world-wide state, but as a world-wide religion. We seem to hear those sacred pages saying, "Long enough have there been local forms held in some Jerusalem, available only after long journeyings; long enough have there been wise men of the temple and the porch who have stood afar from the people, muttering their for the most part obscure soliloquy; long enough have the sibyls sung their ambiguous words from hidden caves whither none but kings or warriors could come. Full time is it for a word that shall go forth to the people, be they of empire or republic, rich or poor, and upon any shore." Such seems the announcement upon the face of the New Testament, and in grand harmony with this professed idea Christ moved from place to place the friend of all; and the apostle to the Gentiles sailed from island to island and land to land, the ambassador to the world. It is said that Paul even crossed Spain, and at the Atlantic coast found, as he supposed, the limits of the world. That broad wave turned him back.

The fact that the Christian Church was first named an *ecclesia* points out not obscurely its ideal scope, for that word had for hundreds of years indicated a convention of the people. The Ecclesia was the Greek house of representatives—a house which stood as a check upon archons and senates, a mediator between the multitude and the ambition of orators and generals. As the public throng was called by heralds who passed along from street to street, the meeting was so named "the called out," or the "ecclesia," and from such associations it has descended to us. Thus all the parts of Christianity—its Christ, its apostles, its avowed object, its ignoring states, its simplicity of doctrine, and its very Church name—confess it to be a religion for the whole people, and hence nothing but a holy crusade against the sins of the wide world.

Such being the avowed design of the founder of this religion, we who profess to believe it are in the path of duty only when we are in sympathy with this large design, and are shaping our thoughts and feelings and actions to this immense scope of the Gospel. We, as a Christian nation and as private Christians, are here to-day in what religious truth we have, only because the religion of Palestine assumed the form of a mission rather than of a local faith. Palestine had held its Hebrew ideas for two thousand years without having sent outward one single chapter from Isaiah or one single psalm from David. Wonderful and divine as was the Deism of the Old Testament compared with the polytheism of the classic states, and sacred as were the hymns of the temple compared with any religious songs of the surrounding lands, yet none of the theology of the Hebrews seems to have broken out of its national confines into the classic world, and not a psalm of David seems ever to have sent its music over to where Homer held a harp, or to where Virgil was devoting his life to a chaste and an elevated poetry. Palestine lay beside Greece for hundreds of years, with only a fragment of the Mediterranean between; and yet between Athens in her glory and Jerusalem in her almost equal splendor, no exchange of creed, or prayer, or hymn seems ever to have taken place. What thoughts these two cities had of each other must have been in the line of wondering when the armies of one might thunder at the gates of the other. The active idea with both was, not how they might spread their poetry, or their psalms and their worship, but how they might advance and support their thrones.

Born into such a spirit, Christianity would have remained in Palestine, just as Hebraism had remained there. But Christ reversed the genius of religion. He separated it from state and attached it to man as a citizen of the world, and moved it from its narrow borders, and from that hour the psalms of David and the songs of the new Church began to cross the sea by every wind that wafted the merchant's ship. It must have been a thrilling passage of eloquence when one of the Roman orators, in perhaps the second century, arose in the public assembly and said: "Your altars and temples are all becoming vacant; your laws are passing away before the temple and laws of this Christ."

The violent deaths suffered by the early apostles and disciples prove that this religion did not confine itself to the home of its birth or attach to the existing temporal powers, but did so cast itself forward as into a wider destiny, that each petty governor feared it as being the embodiment of a most unbridled ambition. Paul so waked up the world by his eloquence that he was put to death at Rome, as though like Cæsar he was reaching forth for a crown; John was banished to Patmos, after having been put to torture; James was hurled from a battlement in Jerusalem, and thus crushed to death; Matthew was put to death in Abyssinia; Simon Zelotes received his crown of martyrdom in Persia; and in Persia, also, Jude was slain by a cruel death; the death of Thomas took place on the coast of Coromandel; Philip was hanged to a pillar in Hierapolis; Andrew was crucified at Patræa in Achaia, and James of Zebede in Asia the Less. Thus in this bloody death-page, where every land is seen to have opened its bosom to receive the mangled form of a disciple, we read in these crimson letters that Christianity is the religion of all which may claim the glory of having taken the whole world into its heart. All these widely separated tombs tell us that from the cross itself the testament religion began at once a march which was to pay no more regard to geographical and national lines that Christ paid when He died for humanity.

How much the Christian philosophy differed from either the Mosaic or the Indian you may infer from the two facts, first that no Hebrew hymn passed over to Greece or Rome in 500 years, though the lands lay upon one small sea and under one sky, and yet in fifty years after Christ his form of religion had penetrated to the British islands. Bishop Stillingfleet says "there is good evidence that the Christian Church was planted in these islands in the first century;" perhaps alluding to the evidence of Eusebius, who says the apostles passed over the ocean and preached in the British isles, and to Theodoret, who says "the Britons embraced the religion of the fishermen and publicans and tent-makers." In the former part of the second century the Gospel had reached Germany, Scythia, Spain, Gaul, and Briton, and in view of this wonderful contagion an orator by the name of Arnobius said: "Is it not a powerful argument that in so short a time the sacraments of Christ are diffused over the world? That orators and rhetoricians, lawyers and philosophers now love this religion and despise what they formerly trusted?"

It would seem from these facts that the religion we cherish was in the very outset a world-religion, not confessing any distinctions of place and people such as have marked all other forms of human worship. The Hebrews looked over their geographical lines with only covetousness or anger; the Chinese built a wall that they might have no intercourse with the multitudes beyond, and calling their own land the "Celestial empire," they despised all other climes; and so all through India it was the effort of thousands of years to build up such a law of caste as would include certain persons in favor and exclude certain others forever. In the very face of all this habit of society, both in its social and political and religious practice, Christianity came as a world-wide creed and worship, the most universal, the most democratic, the most generous, the most God-like of all religions in which the knee has ever bent in prayer.

This missionary spirit, which is bound up in the words of the text and which sent the apostles in all directions spreading out from the tomb of Christ like radiating light from a sun, and which scattered their tombs over all the known world, approached our Canadas and Floridas when the natives were worshiping a devil and pouring out the blood of innocent children each new moon to appease his wrath. When the Spaniards founded their New Spain on the Florida coast, they found the natives offering human sacrifices, and were actually drowning children in the lake to please their horrid deity. Though the Spaniards were seeking only wealth, yet they had with them the Catholic religion, and that Gospel they planted and began at once to overthrow the inhuman customs of the new world.

It was the painful degradation of America and of several lands which travel was bringing into notice, which called to the front such heroes as Xavier in the sixteenth century. You have heard, once before at least, the noble response Xavier made when his friends attempted to alarm him and dissuade him when he was about to sail upon his great mission :

" Hush you ! close your dismal story,
What to me are tempests wild ?
Heroes on their way to glory,
Mind not pastimes for a child.
'Tis for souls of men I'm sailing,
Blow ye winds north, south, east, west ;
Though the storm be round me wailing
There'll be calm within my breast."

It was the advent of a few such heroes that won for the eighteenth century the name of the " Missionary century," but our century has come now to rob the past one of its special fame. That era laid great foundations and our century builds upon its solid rock, thus dividing the honor of the world's evangelization.

Thus stands that great religious work toward which you are asked to contribute your mites to-day, gifts which will perhaps express not your pecuniary ability so much as your thought or care about this vast benevolence among your fellow-men. A gift does not always express one's power, but often only the amount of his information and his sympathy. Thousands give little because they know and care so little about the matter in whose name the offering is made. It ought to be enough of information, the single remembrance, that our religion is all a misssonary action and a missionary result. The condition of this land compared with the old centuries of cruelty is to be credited to the outgoing religion of Jesus that cuts the cables that bound their ships, and sent our fathers hither when the land was a wilderness and the very sky full of wintry storm. It was not the richness of the soil, not the flowing rivers, not the chains of lakes, not the timber of the forests, not the ores in the earth, which have given our country its happiness and varied excellence, for the Indian roamed all over this grand continent, but remained a savage still; it was not civil liberty alone that made us a great people, for the Indians enjoyed the most perfect civil liberty all over this broad prairie and mountain world ; it was rather the religious and ethical ideas which were sent over in the Christian ships that marked out a future nobler than the career of the savage. Money was gathered just as we ask for it to-day, and brave hearts sailed away from home and country, just as now the missionary sails, and that gave us America, just as your gifts and a hundred years will give the world a Christian India or a Christian Chinese Empire.

> " Not as the conquerer comes,
> They, the true-hearted, came
> Not with the roll of stirring drums,
> And the trumpet that sings of fame.
>
> " Not as the flying come
> In silence and in fear ;
> They shook the depths of the deserts gloom,
> With their hymns of lofty cheer."

This poem recalls the cause of American greatness, and the deep foundations of her destiny, but this hymn is nothing else than a repetition of the sentiment that moved Francis Xavier, and Paul, and the divine Master of all.

In our country all this form of benevolence merits a special respect, inasmuch as the Protestant Churches have ignored the distinctions of sects which prevail at home, and for almost a hundred years, dating from the London society, have gone to the benighted lands in the name of great leading truths of Christianity instead of in the name of a multitude of sectarian ideas. Although recently certain fields have been assigned to certain great denominations, yet this has been done in the name of efficiency and economy rather in the name of sectarianism. After the hundred-year experiment, there is no probability that any missionary gold will be exhausted upon any indoctrinational of the heathen world in denominational ideas, for the tendency of the present is to abandon sectarian ideas at home; hence there will be little disposition to inculcate abroad doctrines which are rapidly dying by our own firesides. The Church of England joins with the dissenting Churches in India as a fact, and cares little for the apostolic succession in a land where the Brahmin can so far outdo it in the quality and absurdity of holy touchings and holy pedigrees. And there the Calvinist conceals his five points, for the crowd of Indian philosophers can always propose ten points far more obscure, and thus all the Protestant sects approach the whole pagan world with the Gospel reduced to its simplest expression. Blessed era it will be when we shall be as fully ashamed in America of the things that divide us as we are when our feet touch India or Japan. Can it be possible that it requires home training, that is, local and youthful prejudice, to enable us to see the immense worth of our dogmas, and that approaching foreigners not fully drilled in the sectarian method and tactics we fear their smile of unbelief or derision? It is ominous if, having a score or so of peculiar ideas, we should all get together and agree to say little about them to this Chinaman and that Brahmin. Such a condition of things would seem to indicate one more step along this path, an agreement to say little about these differences to persons not pagans and not upon foreign shores.

We have come to-day to a survey of Christianity in its truest significance, and hence in its wanderings about from race to race, from island to continent, from river to sea, we may learn what are its most essential parts. A student shutting himself up in his room may, from the Bible, elaborate a perfect system which shall omit nothing regarding the human will or the mode and quality of everything, but the world in actual experiment may not need, nor even faintly appreciate, one-tenth part of this closet-made system. But when the Gospel is observed out among men in India and America, there in the faces and life of its votaries one may make out such a true bibical theology as no closet can ever produce. The whole mission work at home and abroad is the best interpretation of Jesus Christ that we can anywhere find, for it determines for us what truths on the sacred page are most valuable for the vast stream of life that is pouring along across earth to eternity. If this spectacle is not badly read it indicates that what the world needs is a perfect combination of Christ as an example and Christ as a mediator, a full confession of man's power and God's power, a full conversion and a high enlightenment. The world reveals three great wants—pardon through Christ, light through Christ, a new heart through the Spirit. Give a soul these, release from its guilt, a new heart for new deeds, new light that its deeds may be right, and it has found the inmost heart of Christianity. Not only does the great mission movement at home and abroad reveal the valuable part of theology, but it declares to us what Christianity is in its essence. It is only a perpetual crusade. It is not a life-long encampment in the midst of luxury and ease, but is a march in search of the happiness and holiness of society. Hence, the great awakenings of the past have come from Christians who were almost homeless and Churchless, who were light-armed and unencumbered, fully out in the world for a campaign. Mankind does not run to a new life from an instinct. Men make long journeyings to fields where diamonds are sown, and to where gold sparkles in the sand, but they do not seek a spiritual religion thus. It makes the journeyings and bears the cross, the hymn and prayer, to Greenland's icy mountain and India's coral strand.

It is the glory of these missionary centuries that they have inaugurated a religion which does not withdraw into a little circle marked out by wealth, or ease, or selfishness, and there wait for a wicked world, and a neglected and unwelcome world, to come and beg to be let into the mercies of Christ hidden by the cruelty of man, but a religion which issues forth from the disgraceful repose of past ages and sings its hymn and offers a loving invitation out in the wide world by every shore, under every sky. The world has seen enough of a religion which wraps itself up in indifference and knows and cares nothing of the human family. Greece had such a type of morals, Rome had such a form of spiritual death ; and enough has the world had of religion that was bound to state and had no destiny but that of empire ; and ready now is society for a Christlike faith that goes forth like the perfume of roses free to child and king alike, a fragrance which climbs over walls and out of palace windows, and mounting into the chariot of the summer wind crosses the field of the poor laborer and the highway of the traveler, a breath from heaven, an emblem of God's grace.

THE WORLD'S GREAT NEED.*

PROF. DAVID SWING.

Ye must be born again.—*John* iii. 7.

The great pursuit of the wisest, and best men that have ever lived has been to help onward, and upwards the morals of the people. By common consent the names of Socrates, Seneca, Marcus Aurelius, Luther, Calvin, Knox, Penn, George Fox, are the grandest of names. Beside such stars of fame, the lustre of a captain in bloody war, or of a Cresus, or Rothschild, fades away as glow-worms at sunrise. Nations have always looked with love, and confidence upon their moralists. Mark the Chinese love for Confucius, and American love for the morals of Washington, and Franklin. There is a common feeling that in such men lie the reasons for national success, and the basis of security. Out of them seem to issue the nation's moral life, as the tree grows from rich soil.

Now what is it that exalts these few moralists? What is it that determines at once that such men are the jewels of their century, or State?

Morals do not please as does music, painting, or eloquence. Morals do not make us laugh, or weep; and hence Paul, and Daniel, and Luther, and Fox must be lifted up in the world's esteem by some new, and peculiar kind of fact.

It seems to me we find this fact in the public conviction of the utter depravity of the masses, and in the public approval of any soul that can, or will help a depraved race upward. Paul is loved the more because the world feels deeply that such morals are a stranger to it, and yet are its only hope. Suppose the world to have been quite free from sin, Paul's moralizing would have been without significance. Martyn's trip to Persia would have been only the roamings of a traveler.

It is the world's confessed wickedness, it is the world's universal, and inborn depravity that makes the Christian, and

*A sermon preached in Standard Hall by Prof. David Swing, pastor of the Fourth Presbyterian Church — (destroyed by the fire).

moral leaders flame like suns in the human sky. The fame of every such man as Paul, or Socrates, or Seneca is a public confession of depravity. Those men are thrown up by a great want. Their fame is the confession of old sorrow, old grief, old tears. It is the awful fact of universal sin that renders these names so precious. Their wreaths are woven by the fingers of Sorrow. What rendered the life, and words of Marcus Aurelius so beautiful? It was the fact that not a living mortal known to the whole Roman world had lived, or could live after that fashion. He was bright by reason of the dark background.

It is not worth while, therefore, to quarrel with the Bible when it says, "I was born in iniquity;" "the heart is deceitful;" "the heart is desperately wicked;" and "man must be born again." The conspicuousness of Christ, of Paul, of Penn, of the great Elliott among the Indians shows that the Bible is only a picture of human life, and that men do need to "be born again." You may quarrel with theologians if you wish, who have taken Bible texts into their labratories, and have re-appeared after long stirring of the crucible having in their hands some strange compound of mysterious color, and questionable use; but with the plain Bible — with its words, "Ye must be born again"— let us have no debate. It was the effort of the old chemists to turn all things into gold, but the old theologians seemed to have possessed the faculty of changing gold into all things else; and taking a pure, priceless truth from the Bible were wont, unconscious of its worth, to join it to their amalgam, and then emerge with a poor oroid — their very faces meanwhile crying out the old, "Eureka." With these, one may dispute, but as for the simple words of the Bible, they are the picture of the world's facts. They are the mirror, which reflects back to us nothing but our face with no deformity, or charm left out. Those words are deeply written on all the generations, and their meaning is only too vivid. It makes the heart, and the head to ache. Let us confess that one of the most prominent facts of society is its moral weakness, its depravity. It *ought* to "be born again."

It is generally assumed that a child is born with certain mental predispositions; with a gift for language, for mechanics, for poetry, for reasoning. Hence it was said thousands of years ago, "A poet is not made by study, he is born." The great English dramatist says, "How hard it is to hide the sparks of nature." Another says, "Nature may lie hid for a time, but at last she will reveal herself." Thus it has always been assumed, that when one is born he is hurled into a certain orbit where he must journey forever, as calmly, and resistlessly as the planets.

This sentiment is not true to the letter, but it shows what Christ meant when He said, "Ye must be born again." He meant that the soul must be hurled into being a second time. Its first life was a failure. It ought to be reborn so that a new genius, a new drift might be possible.

Oh! what a vast change is here indicated — a change in the depths of our nature — a tearing down and re-building of the very soul.

Now the world's greatest *fact* being its degradation, its greatest *want* is to be expressed by the word "recreation," or "reborn."

This is the world's great *want.* It is its *greatest* want — this reconstruction of the human soul so that it will no longer love to lie, nor cheat, nor sin in any form, but will love God, and all moral beauty. Even old Egypt, thousands of years ago taught her citizens that after death the soul stood before God, and a Council of two and forty just men, and had to make the following statement: "I have not blasphemed. I have not stolen. I have not stirred up strife. I have not slandered any one. I have not practiced any crime. I have given food to the hungry, drink to the thirsty, clothes to the naked." Unless the soul could make this statement truly, it was at once stricken from existence; but if it could make this statement truly it went to heaven. These creeds Champollion has deciphered from old carved rocks unread for years, far in the thousands.

Yes, the great want of earth is a society living in honor, and virtue; loving God, and mankind. Such a result would be Heaven. To approach it, and finally reach it, is the mission of religion.

There are several Christian sects that do not sufficiently magnify this idea of conversion, or new life. They believe in it, but do not make it the great central thought of their teaching. With the Methodists, and Presbyterians, and their kindred schools, the first effort is to help convert men, and and hence their great question to the candidate for membership is, "Do you feel that you have undergone a change of heart; do you hate sin; do you love holiness?" And persons enter the Church, or remain out, according to the responses to these inquiries. It matters not if some assert a change who have really met with none, and if some assert a falsehood knowingly. The questions are exactly in the line of the world's reform; they are the great questions to be asked, and hence the religion that most patiently asks them, and most lovingly seeks affirmative answers, will always secure better results than a Church that passes them by in silence, and assumes that all is well in the soul.

The perpetual effort to build up a new spiritual life, the unchanging conviction that soul needs a profound reform now, and the accompanying belief that such a new drift of being may be found by the heart, has all the advantage to be found in all direct effort toward a result. The pure rationalist will assure you, that the quantity of education, or wealth in a land will be, as the quantity of zeal, and longing, and will-power in those two directions. We are informed, that the good elocution of a Greek orator, was the result of long conflict with a natural foe, and that the culture of all Greece, was the result of a national zeal along one narrow channel of feeling, and thought. From the universality of such facts, has grown up the maxim that "the gods help those who help themselves." In a world subject to such a law, it is cruel to strike from religion the intense longing for a new heart, and the absorbing belief in its necessity, and then wait for moral progress to come in by some unknown gate.

It has counted wonderfully in the race of usefulness that the Methodists, for example, have for one hundred years, turned their longings, and efforts toward the immediate reconstruction of the human spirit. Notwithstanding the weakness of shoutings, and the frequent discord in their old hymns, the long pursuit of a better life has given at last to our land, millions of the best citizens. The Presbyterians present a similar spectacle. Guilty often of fanaticism—guilty of midnight meetings, and of falling to the floor in the struggle with the old Satan, they have nevertheless surpassed rationalistic methods in the great work of recasting the soul. In some of the villages of Persia, there is to-day a sudden, and vast reform taking place under the mission banners, in the name of the actual pursuit of a regenerate heart. What men seek, they find. Only that gate opens at which men knock.

It is useless to reply, "We do not believe in a miraculous conversion of the soul, but only in a conversion brought about by study, will-power, hymns, and prayer;" for it is of a change of *heart* only I speak. I have said nothing about the agent in the new creation. The pure rationalists believe in a "changed" heart, and would seem bound, therefore, to make this "new heart" a vital thing in their Church life. For it is the world's greatest want, its greatest longing, its only hope. Some orthodox sects pursue with more zeal this one object—the transformation of the heart—and hence seem to be more in the path of the highest human duty—more fully in the path of reform.

From Dr. Ryder's* letters, you will perceive that his philoso-

* Referring to a correspondence in the *Chicago Tribune* between Wm. Ryder, D.D., of St. Paul's (Universalist) Church, and E. O. Burgess, D.D., of the Christian Church, growing out of a sermon preached by the former on Rev. George H. Hepworth's renunciation of Unitarianism.

phy believes in a new heart, but in securing this new heart, instead of increasing the labor, and whole pressure in *this* life, he prolongs the time. He diminishes the power, and doubles the time. He allows us future centuries upon the other shore in which to come to a harmony with God. But the orthodox limit us to a few years here, and hence pursue with more enthusiasm, and with deepest feeling the work of reforming their fellow men. They shorten the time, and double the impulse; and when we remember that what this world needs is good men on this side of the grave, rather than saints on the other, we cannot but feel that orthodoxy is the best friend of the life that now is. When we consider that the great enemy of society is sin, the religion that makes a change of heart its chief object, seems evidently the better one for the great end. Only those efforts count in the progress of the centuries, which harmonize with the world's great need—which become parts of God's work—parts of the development and growth of humanity.

It is to be admitted that education, books, art, reason help to convert the soul—to change it—hence all enlightened pulpits are full of usefulness. But when to these influences a Church adds an additional effort, pointed and urgent to convert the heart, it may well claim a special usefulness. A Church will be useful according to the depth of its realization that men must "be born again"—not hereafter, but in these passing days.

Let us come now to a comparison of the means for creating, or producing this new heart.

There are sects that expect a new heart to come from the common means of civilization. A new heart as to sin, is just like a new taste as to learning, or music—a simple result of culture. They call in no special agents, no superhuman influence.

The truly orthodox, to the influence of all natural means, add the special influence of God's Spirit, and of a divine Christ. In the very outset one might conjecture that a religion claiming help from God, and from a divine Savior, would most sowerfully affect the heart. None of the influences of civilization are left out, but in addition to these the heart opens up a communion with God; opens up a study, and soul-communion with Jesus Christ, and thus casts itself into the presence of infinite purity, power, justice, and goodness. What are the ordinary forces of civilization compared with such a fellowship as this? The element to be eliminated from man is sin. Now civilization bears within itself a great remnant of sin. Civilization is not holy. It is not infinitely just, and pure. But the Spirit of God is the very opposite of sin. The soul, therefore, coming to God, comes to perfect purity, and sees its own wickedness as it can never see it in human culture. Before this soul-communion with God, the influence of human agencies fades in feebleness.

It may be that, here and there, an individual might seek moral perfection, without being influenced by the idea of God. In sober years, here and there, a soul might seek what might be called morals, as being a refined temperance of life. I think Stuart Mill has said, he could imagine a religion of humanity, where man would seek uprightness from a love of himself, and of society's peace; but these possible theories, count nought in presence of the sweeping fact, that all morals have revolved around the idea of God. God renders virtue necessary, and beautiful, and is to be its reward. As the eyes of servants look unto the hand of their masters, as the eyes of the maiden unto the hand of her mistress, so our eyes, wait upon the Lord our God, until He have mercy upon us.

While God is Creator of material worlds, yet the heart feels that they are but decorations of His temple, and that the rational soul is the chief end of the world in its height, and depth. Hence the greatest relation of Deity, is the relation to the soul. Hence God must be the God of morals more extremely than the God of matter. If, as Hamilton says, "there is nothing great on earth but man, and nothing great in man except his soul," so we suspect, that there is nought so great in the sky as God, and no attribute in that blessed One so vast, as His moral beauty. When, therefore, the heart thinks of its sin, it must at once, in fear, or in hope, feel the weight, sweet, or sorrowful, of that sinless One, all around like the air, or sunshine.

In seeking a new moral nature, the soul must fly to this vast bosom, and seek its new life there —

> "Go when the morning shineth,
> Go when the noon is bright,
> Go when the eve declineth,
> Go in the hush of night."

Hence, when we seek the conversion of the human race, give me that religion which leads the wicked heart up to a communion direct with God, and with Jesus Christ. Where God is, there is no sin; and the heart that believes most in God, and looks most to Him for help, will become separated most widely from the love, and pursuit of vice.

It is an attribute of human nature, that it is educated by objects outside of self. Before each scholar, there stand some great scholars of the past alluring, and detaining, and transforming the mind of to-day. We are all lesser lights, revolving around some central sun of immense light, and heat. Without this influence we make no progress.

In religion it is not otherwise, and hence, most useful must be that form that makes of Christ a divine Being, and invites the heart to move about such a centre of power, holiness, and love. Its theory would seem at the outset to promise most for society. The moment you declare Christ only a human being, you have weakened His influence upon the soul. The lignt, and warmth are eclipsed, and the poor soul gropes about, and tries to find in civilization a power denied it in the realm of the divine, and infinite. To part with ignorance, let us go to the learned; to part with sin, let us go to the presence of the holy.

As the planets get further from the sun their light, and heat diminish. Their flowers, and fruits lose sweetness; their summers shorten. What must it be in the most remote Neptune—three hundred times as far away as our earth! Oh, star of perpetual ice, and winter; without bird, or flower, or leaf! But to chill the central sun would give the same result. Now in the soul's universe, there is a scene as dreary. Christ is declared to be only man—only fallible man. And thus the human race is crowded back, far away from the old centre of Divine warmth, and light; and many is the soul which this theory has left without a flower, or leaf, or trace of summer time.

Mr. Hepworth excites hope only in this, that he has kindled a little better central sun for his heart—has declared Christ to be Divine, above other measure of divinity believed in by many of his sect. He redoubles the radiance, and the warmth of that character that has always shone in rejuvenating, converting power upon the heart. Men looking upon civilization, or culture only, may not be reborn in spirit; but looking upon a divine Christ in love, their souls are affected by the holiness, and immortal life in the great vision.

Instead of man's revolving around humanity, Mr. Hepworth invites him to revolve about the Divine. It is a step upward, but not an espousal of orthodoxy, not even a departure from the old Unitarian Creed. To preach fully his gently orthodox ideas it seemed not necessary to withdraw from associations long and sacred; able in themselves to clothe his words with power—for the creed of his denomination embraces his ideas in its grandest books, and many are the hearts in his Society that are willing that the soul of Channing should come back to the half-desolate home. I feel that there are thousands in the Unitarian body who are willing, even anxious, to have a common, fallible man plucked from the centre of their system, and to see replaced there a divine Savior, drawing all hearts by His love, and heavenly attributes.

The world will, sooner or later, be compelled to go to the Divine presence — not to human presence — for its new heart. Mankind has not holiness enough to entice any heart from its sins — has not love enough to persuade, nor power enough to alarm. It is the conception of an ever-present God; it is the sublime divinity of Jesus; it is communion with these characters; it is a belief in the infinite love, and power, and justice, and in the all-pervading presence of Deity, that can give to this world noble, converted hearts, and can bear earth along toward the new birth — the new genius of human life.

THE GRADUAL DECLINE OF VICE.*

DAVID SWING.

"It shall be more tolerable for the land of Sodom and Gomorrah."—*Matthew x: 15.*

The names of these two cities, over whose ruins the Dead sea is supposed to roll its bitter waves, are read before you this morning as words that may remind you that the present is not the only age of vice, but that great sins lie back of our times. I announce as my theme "The Decline of Vice." The discourse before you last Sunday closed with an appeal to you to gird up your strength against the evils of the age; but that we may all possess some general, truthful view of the work on hand, of its magnitude and despair or hope, it seems desirable that an hour should be given to inquiry as to the present attitude of human depravity compared with the long yesterday. This inquiry may lead us along two paths, the one leading through the *a priori* question, What should be the result of the increase of knowledge? The other leading through the actual facts with the question, What has been the history of sin? The relation between knowledge and virtue is, as a general truth, the relation between a cause and an effect. While no one will contend that knowledge will fully regenerate the heart and make a saint out of a sinner, yet the tendency of information is to raise the individual to a higher plane of morality. Our penitentiaries, and also our observation, teach us that ignorance is the mother of vice. Says an old Greek, "Better to be unborn than untaught, for ignorance is the root of misfortune." The great Robert Hall said, "Ignorance gives an eternity to prejudice; a perpetuity to error." The majority of convicts in the dungeon or upon the scaffold cannot write, but use that fatal emblem called "his mark." All through the Scriptures virtue is represented as a light, and sin as a darkness, and in obedience to this distinction, Satan is the prince of darkness and Christ the light of the world. Every motion man makes is along the line of his information, it being the great path maker for him in the wilderness, his pillar of fire and cloud in all his long journeying.

If you find an Indian planting a few seeds in wild Oregon, or setting forth with his spear to kill fish, or with his treacher-

* Sermon delivered in the Fourth Presbyterian Church, March 29, 1874.

ous arrow to attack his enemy, he is moving along the lines of his information, and he will use all his light about planting his maize, or spearing the fish, or waylaying the white man. Over his dead enemy he will shed no tears, for he knows nothing of a golden rule, and nothing of the rights of man or the sacredness of life. All moralists or causists so feel the causal relation between ignorance and crime that they hold the heathen world to be responsible for not having sought such light as might have improved their virtue, thus confessing that the order of nature is "light" and then "virtue." When a mind like that of William Penn, or Richard Cobden, has made a study of man, and has looked into the rights of life, liberty, and the pursuit of happiness, it becomes incapable of the atrocities which give actual pleasure to the untutored Modoc of the West. Penn and Cobden are rays of light upon the heart, emblems of that softening of soul which God's great truth always brings.

God's moral world and His physical world being covered all over with a net-work of laws as numerous and delicate as the tenderest webs in the spider's web, the first equipment for living in this world is a wide information as to these laws of body, and mind, and society, and religion. A knowledge of these is the sun which must turn night into day, and sleep into life.

It is now seen that under the increase of knowledge in the medical art, the average of human life has risen, and is now ascending. The relation of air, and exercise, and food, and sleep, to health has been so studied from the standpoint of science and experiment, that this new light pouring around the body lengthens its years, and makes them not only longer, but happier. But God's world being all founded upon the same fundamental law, information will play the same part in morals that it performs in the medical art, and will tend to add to the quantity of virtue as truly as the study of pathology has extended the human lease of life. In such vast empires as India and China, where murder, and theft, and infanticide are customs allied to those of religion in a wonderful, but senseless partnership, the entrance of light alone, omitting any religious principle, has gone as far toward checking the bad customs as the new steam plow in Turkey has gone toward supplanting the old crooked stick that was once dragged through the fields. It is a great mistake to suppose that all the ills of mankind come from their not being religious or conscientious, and that all the human family needs is a sudden conversion to our Christianity. Conversion will only check those actions which the mind knows to be wrong, but will only add fuel to a line of bad conduct, which the mind supposes to be right. Religious conversion brings only an increased desire to follow the right, but it does not designate a new right for the mind. Hence, in the dark ages, a religious revival among the Catholics was always attended by a new slaughter of Protestants, because the new zeal in the heart did not bring any new information to the intellect, but only fanned the existing ideas into flame. What is demanded along with a well-disposed heart is a well-informed intellect. However good a man may be, it will be perfectly impossible for him to escape a vice unless he knows it to be such, and hence information or knowledge is an absolute condition of morality or manhood. The opium-eaters among the lowest classes in China, and the dirt eaters and whisky drinkers among the Indian tribes, do not descend from an origin of sin only, but from an ancestry of ignorance. Their noble life will come not simply from a study of religion, but also from a study of physiology and all the laws of health and refinement. Men are bad enough through sin, but they are wretched beyond this through ignorance. In India the most devout fakirs, who live for nothing but God and the soul, will once a day roll in the mud, or in the foulest gutter, in order to show their contempt for the sinful thing called the body. Now what those fakirs need is not an increase of religion, but an increase of sense. They need to learn that sin is not in the body, but in the soul, and that the true God is not a being worshiped by a beastly conduct, by a wallowing in the mire, but by a noble, perfect soul in a pure, perfect body. When Christ forgave His murderers, on the ground that they *knew not what they did*, He reaffirmed for us the proposition that much of the world's sin and evil comes from an ignorance that thinks in the midst of awful actions that it is doing God's service. It serves Satan under the supposition that he is God. The evils of the world are wider than the direct desire of mankind to commit sin, for millions do wrong supposing it to be right; hence, in order to find some foundation as broad as this dreadful superstructure, we must combine ignorance and wickedness, and then we have the base adequate for the fabric.

Having thus found that ignorance is a vast cause of the world's great evils, we infer from the gradual spread of intelligence that the great vices are on the gradual decline. If the cause is declining we need no *a posteriori* inquiry to show us that the effect must be so far on the wane. If the supply of food has failed in India, we need not wait ninety days in order to learn the effects from the actual dying beds of mothers and children; and if a rich harvest soon comes, we need not wait to learn the result from the strong men in the streets next summer, and from the ringing laughter of children. God's world is so unbending in its relation of cause and effect that the moment a cause is abated one jot you may assume an equal abatement in the result. Now, much of the evil of society coming from ignorance, we may, so far as ignorance is being dispelled, congratulate the world upon a decline of its moral sorrows.

Having thus alluded to the influence of increased knowledge, the question that remains is, Has human knowledge increased? Has ignorance been modified? Has this plague been somewhat abated? We think that no one will deny that knowledge has gradually increased in those nations which have in twenty-five hundred years spread out from the Mediterranean. Light steadily advanced in the Hebrew nation from Abraham to Daniel; and from the Greek and Roman starting points down through the great nations of Europe and America, information in all departments has been steadily amassed and handed down from one era to the next. Especially in the last three centuries has all truth become an object of pursuit and love; and hence every science, from politics to chemistry; every inquiry, from the rights of the throne to the most practical physiology; every theory of health, from a study of health to a study of exercise, has been unfolded in new breadth and new affection. The sciences of chemistry, and physiology, and hygiene have marshaled their startling truths in front of the great vices of the social evil, and intemperance of drink and of food, and have battled them for a hundred years, and the attack increases in fierceness each generation. Hence, if there be some relation between ignorance and vice, that ought to be abating the vice which is confessedly so abating the ignorance.

But we behold another great light shining down from the Mediterranean shore, a light better than the stars that shone from the sky of Greece and the sky of Italy. While all information in Christianity, or politics, or philosophy, has its secret influence in favor of virtue, yet it must be confessed that a knowledge of all the high duties of man, man as related to self, and to friends, and to society, and to God, is of all the best, and if any truth will check sin, that relating to duty and soul and God must be that powerful knowledge. Looking back we see a star that makes all others fade. Its light, radiating out from nothing but a manger in the outset, and from a rude cross at last, has for eighteen hundred years diffused itself all over the Western hemisphere, embracing Russia, Germany, France, England, America, all as a mother throws her arms around the children who were lost but are found. Christianity set forth, not as a conversion alone, but also as a light for the mind. Pontius Pilate may have been sincere, but he was ignorant of duty, and weak in its moral attributes. Christianity moved upon the world not as a simple zeal, but as a light, and hence, if to know what the body is, and what the soul is, and what earth is, and what death is, what heaven and hell may be; if to have some just conception of God, if to hold some correct view of our neighbor and all the reciprocal duties of life, if to know the golden rule and that the pure in heart shall see God, are truths of any value, then Christianity comes as the profoundest information which has ever burst through the clouds and shone down upon the world of man. Looking upon Christ as a moral light, and looking as far as a feeble intellect can grasp such an effulgence, we ought to conclude that vice has suffered a shock in that so much of its foundation of ignorance has been swept away. But we reminded you that evil had two elements in its foundation, the one ignorance, the other hostility to the truth, even when well known. Christianity attacks both these foundations of evil, and works equally with the intellect and the heart, revealing duty and making the soul love duty.

Seeing, therefore, a gradual increase of knowledge from the great Eastern sources, Greece, Rome, and Palestine, and seeing this knowledge spreading out westward in all that varied magnificence of science and gospel, of crucible and cross, of body and soul, of human liberty and divine love, and then remembering the invention of printing which has poured this varied wisdom into every house as sunlight pours into the window, I must reach the conclusion that the vices of the civilized world ought to be on the decline. There are agencies abroad in the world which appear adequate to a reduction of the quanity of wickedness.

Our second inquiry was designated as being a survey of the actual facts in the case. Having seen what the spread of light ought to accomplish, we may inquire whether there has been any such moral achievement. First, let me warn you against supposing that the loud outcry now raised on all sides against every form of vice and dishonor, indicates that evil is on the advance and goodness on the decline, for the present turmoil proves only that the public sense has progressed so far that it will no longer submit silently to great wrongs and follies. The judgment and the moral and prudential senses have been so developed in the past, especially in the recent past, that silence is no longer possible. What former ages endured easily because of the feeble public light and public conscience, raises now a vast uproar when seen in the new light and morals of the passing century. The great emancipation war which raged in our land from 1830 to 1860 did not arise from the new barbarism of slavery, for, as a fact, bondage had not grown more inhuman, but arose from the fact that an old evil had encountered a new intellectual and moral development, and hence came the great conflict. It is with such reflections we look upon the present conflict over intemperance and the social evil. These monsters have not absolutely gained in vice and ferocity, but the public conscience has grown until it has not the indifference to vice which marked the world when kings lived for glory and pleasure, and nobles for banquets and the fox chase. These monsters, which we call by the general name of vice, have been dragging their foul lengths along over hundreds of years, and much of battle is located in our time, because it has so gathered light from reason and Christianity that it can no longer endure such great wrongs. The sin has been stationary, but the public impatience has advanced.

Leaving these suggestions to the judgment of each of you, it remains to allude only in a brief manner to the historical facts in the case. Whoever would deduce any conclusions regarding the moral progress of society, must deal only in long periods, for earth is a star whose physical days are indeed composed of twenty-four hours, but whose moral days are each as a thousand years. Coming up out of God's eternity, where ages sink like snow-drops in the ocean, our earth brought with it this awful disregard of time, and makes little count of the days of you and me, looks upon a summer and a winter as only grains of sand upon its mighty shore; and all our three-score years sink into its mighty life as autumn leaves fall upon the mountain side and are only received tenderly into its mold, but create no jar in the wide and deep foundations of adamant. To estimate the morals of the human family, to mark an increase or decrease of sin, you must look away from this day, this year, this generation, and so far as possible behold all the impressive spectacle that reaches from the old Eden to the newest America.

What was that past? The words Sodom and Gomorrah recall at once some of the early forms of the world's corruption. The vices of that period, as revealed in the history and conduct of Lot, were not the incidental vices of a savage tribe, but the vices of the most civilized nations, for the Hebrew commonwealth, as far as the age of David and Solomon, repeated the sins of Sodom, only upon a diminishing scale, and thus was a mirror, not of barbarism, but of the best type of old civilization. The history of Egypt is a history of mingled science and splendor and sin. The Egyptians actually worshiped gods of vice, and in all respects equaled the reputation of Sodom and Gomorrah for indescribable depravity. The exhuming of Herculaneum and Pompeii has lifted a veil from the customs of the Greek and Roman worlds, for those two civilizations were combined there, and there at that mountain's base those two cities sat while nature suddenly embalmed them for far-off generations. The excavations there reveal equally old wealth and old vice, art and dishonor, a cultivated intellect and a darkened conscience, a light upon canvas and marble, but little light upon the soul.

Passing by the notorious immorality or impurity of the Greek and Roman and Egyptian lands, look upon some features of those ages not so commonly alluded to in these surveys of antiquity. Slavery was universal. The rights of man as man were unknown. The Greeks knew the rights of Greeks; the Romas the rights of Romans; but neither knew the rights of man. Hence, no citizen did anything which a slave might do. If pecuniarily possible, the literary man lay upon a lounge while slaves wrote down his thoughts, or brought and took away a volume, or prepared a glass of fragrant wine. Marriage was a frail partnership, and the courtesan often more honored by statesmen than the more refined, home-loving wife. The amphitheatres were a full blossoming of the ignorance of the rights of man, and of the absence of mercy from the heart. In days when ten thousand innocent men were dying in one reign, in presence of eighty thousand spectators, composed of the best citizens of Rome, Cicero was justifying the bloody spectacle; and in one instance when no exhibitions had been given for a time, a petition was sent to the district governor, or prefect, that he would order a show at the amphitheatre, and he graciously said "that not to grant their request would be cruelty."

All through this Roman splendor parents held the power of life and death over their children, and infanticide was very common; and next in cruelty to that was the exposing of infants, under the law that whoever found the exposed child could claim it as his slave forever. Its chance was for death or bondage. Mothers who did not choose either of these barbarous resorts, could sell their infants into bondage in open market.

Lecky says the classic religion exerted no influence upon public morals, for when it taught any valuable truth there was no religious zeal that would nourish the truth into life. At your leisure, my friends, look into the picture of Roman and Greek life, and you will rise from the study thankful that you live in even this wicked city, and that between your home and antiquity the light of a new knowledge and a new religion has fallen in heavenly beauty. As to the great special vices, intemperance and the social evil, which so injure our land, it ought to cheer the heart that these powerful foes are only two out of a large host which once attacked society, and that these two are feebler than they were a hundred years ago. The social evil was almost universal in Europe from Cæsar to Napoleon. Montaigne says there were no virtuous men in his day, and, indeed, we all know that the social vice has swept over the old world as no pestilence or war ever desolated its cities and homes. As to the use of drinks, it may be said that abstinence was almost undreamed of before our generation, and an intemperate use of liquors, from ale to distilled drinks, is as old as the genius that invented the villainies.

We need not descend into particulars. You can recall them. Called upon as you are to contend to-day against the vices of our land, you all seem fully authorized to feel that knowledge and religion do gradually wear away these hard rocks, and give the world a better soil for the moral growth of this generation and its children and the myriads to come. God is no more in the law of gravitation than He is in the laws of reform, and hence as the Niagara has cut its deep ravine back from Queenstown, so the moral power of education and religion are as surely carving a channel through the mass of wickedness on earth. God's word, His truth, will not return unto Him void. As the sun's heat always melts the snow of our fields, and always will while sun and snow continue, so the word of truth spoken by anyone anywhere always will add something to the progress of mankind. God is not only immutable in the law of chemistry and all physics, but in the laws of His love, and if His children assail ignorance with truth and sin with conscience, every movement of the humblest Christian will record itself for good in the bosoms of those that come after the record. Let us look at these great facts and always be of good heart, for although viewed by itself alone, the present looks dark in its sinfulness, and although the efforts of Church and press seem powerless, yet looking away from our few years and reading the changes of society as recorded upon the centuries, we plainly perceive that every good word and deed of each day is embalmed in the great brain and bosom of mankind. As each tree helps make the green of the distant forest and does its part in the impenetrable shade, so the truth of all lips to-day and the prayer of each heart are, in some manner unseen to us but seen of God, handed down to those who shall come when your lips and heart are dust. To a child looking upon the cold sky of March it seems impossible that spring and summer are coming, or can come, but the older mind looks beyond the single morning, looks beyond April and May, and beholds in June a continent covered with waving grasses and trees, and in soft morning air dripping with dew-drops from Maine to Oregon. Thus gradually mankind advances toward an era when the banner of knowledge and the banner of the cross shall wave over every city, and light and love and virtue shall be in every soul. Such a destiny is read in the nature of man and in the character of God.

A RELIGION OF WORDS.*

DAVID SWING.

Not every one that saith unto me Lord, Lord, shall enter into the kingdom of heaven, but he that doeth the will of my Father which is in heaven. *Matthew vii : 21.*

Spirituality is one of the highest stages of civilization, and therefore comes latest in the course of human development. Material associations are the first, hence man first makes up his language and his pantheon of gods out of the solid substances that surround him. The first man was of the earth, earthy; the second man was the Lord from heaven. That is first which is natural, and afterward that which is spiritual. And as man has borne the image of the earthy, so shall he bear the image of the heavenly. The first Adam was made a living soul ; the second Adam a quickening spirit.

In this great transition from the material to the spiritual, years are consumed in the life of the most earnest individual, and in the advance of society in this path a thousand years count only a little. The most sincere heart escapes from materialism so slowly, and so slowly resolves itself and its God into a quickening spirit, that an infinitely long existence would seem to be foreshadowed in this leisurely evolution. To that which grows slowly we attribute long time. The glacier and the accumulating shore of the sea, and the vast oaks of the Pacific slope ask us to allow them long periods in which to have developed their peculiar plan. So the slowness of human unfolding asks us to grant to the individual and to society a vast field called immortality. Instead of drawing only sadness from this tedious march we also find in it an assurance that there are many years beyond.

But our theme for the hour is that a spiritual religion comes last in human experience, and before it comes a religion of things and of words. To offer things to God was earth's first form of being religious. The old temples were full of bows, arrows, shields, helmets and jewels put away from human use

*Preached in McVicker's Theatre to the Fourth Presbyterian Church, by the Pastor, Rev. David Swing.

by a solemn gift-making to the gods. Horace reveals the fact in one of his poems that the sailor rescued from drowning, hung up in the temple what he wore on his body when the divinity rescued him from the grave. A gift was the only known acknowledgment. Different cities vied with each other in making their gods rich. What gold! what garments, what jewels, what armor in the temple of Juno, and what luxuries there were in the temple of Jupiter!

The Athenians, upon the eve of a battle, vowed to Apollo that if he would grant them success they would offer to him as many kids as there were slain of the enemy on the field of battle, and so bloody was their success that the classic nation did not possess flocks enough to meet the vow of the worshippers, and the state funded, as it were, the promise, and offered five hundred a year through successive generations.

Worship was thus conducted by offerings. From baskets of fruits and flowers to thousands of valuable sheep and oxen, gifts were heaped upon the altars. At the dedication of his temple which was itself a costly present to Jehovah, Solomon sacrificed twenty-two thousand oxen and one hundred and twenty thousand sheep as an offering to Him who had brought them out of the land of Egypt and out of the house of bondage. All the earth was covered with this religion of gifts. Hindoo and African, Jew and Gentile, Indian and Roman, Parthian and Greek, accomplished the life of religion by offering some things to their favorite deity.

Good came from the custom, for, that spiritual worship is the highest form of religion, does not make useless or harmful a form full of material things and ideas. The gift-making worship only takes a second position, inferior, but not useless nor absurd. In Solomon's days not to offer a lamb to Jehovah was to be an infidel, for the religious thought and feeling of the times flowing in that channel, the heart that made no offering was an infidel heart. Each age has its own atheist and infidel fashioned out of its own shape of life. Solomon's vast offerings, aside from any relation to a coming Calvary, were, in the current hour, an act of religion, just as an imperfect song is music to those who love it, or as a rude log-hut is a sweet home to those, perhaps half-starved and half-clothed children, who have lived only by its door-sill and its hearth. To laugh at what others possess and to base that laugh upon the superiority of what is our own, is often a mild form of ignorance and self-conceit. Each age has drawn honey out of its own flowers, even if the flowers were wild and of pale single leaf. A gift was a surrender of self, a confession of dependence and a first leaf of charity.

The gift-worship at last passed away. Christ long borne in

such an earthly casket outgrew the narrow confines and appeared in fullness and broad liberty. In Palestine, the religion of gifts terminated virtually in the Sermon upon the Mount, and in the marvellous spiritual life of Jesus. The gift of himself ended the whole gift idea by divine appointment, and by its excessive grandeur, and the purely spiritual philosophy of Christ and His apostles flying on the wings of the Roman language, and Roman fame and power, passed over the world in a circling, rapid flight. All the ends of the earth had felt the Roman power of arms, of letters, of law, of genius, of energy, so that Christianity, climbing into the chariot of Rome, was rapidly borne to all human hearts within the civilized empires of that era. Gifts disappeared from all the temples, lambs and oxen from all the altars, and religion began to resolve itself into a prayer, and penitential tear, and a faith and a hope.

While property measured the value of man and of his god, the surrender of it by man was the most obvious form of service, and the favor of heaven was bought not by a change of human character, but by a bestowal of human goods.

With the uprising of Christ, religion began to withdraw from presents to the Deity and betake itself to the heart. "Blessed are the pure in heart." "Blessed are they that hunger and thirst after righteousness." "The hour cometh and now is when the true worshipper shall worship the Father in spirit and in truth for the Father seeketh such to worship Him." "The hour cometh when ye shall neither in this mountain nor yet in Jerusalem worship the Father."

In this second state of religion a new heart became the chief object to be reached, and rewards from God were promised, not to him who would bring richest presents, but to him who would bring the purest life. But mankind was not ready for this cardinal idea. At least mankind will do nothing hastily. It will not pass to perfection in a day. It will not suffer itself to be hurried, but, like the glacier, must have its own rate of speed — the inseparable trait of its character. No voice has ever found instantaneous obedience. A spiritual religion announced, and a spiritual religion accepted, are different matters. A divine being and a few followers may announce one, but the world is always far below the leading divine souls, and hence after heavenly words are announced it will continue for a time in paths much like those of yesterday. A resemblance is demanded.

From a religion of gifts the world soon hastened to a Christianity of words. Words were the outward sign and in that the heart paused. There were a few generations of simple piety such as St. John revealed, but the measurement of Christianity was soon found in the propositions to which one was willing to subscribe.

Words are the forerunners only of deeds. They are heralds that announce a coming king, but the king's chariot is slow. Hence when you find in the times of Cæsar or Louis XIV., or Calvin, the finest statements about purity and charity, that is no sign that there was any public purity or charity. They had simply been announced, just as a vessel has been signaled when it is yet far out at sea, and perhaps falling back before storms. Words precede actions often by a thousand years. And thus the Sermon on the Mount is not so much man's law as man's prophecy. The world is grand, not when a prophecy is uttered, but when the fulfillment comes.

Millions were finally put to death in the long Christian centuries when they would not repeat the words of the party in power. Honesty of life, religious devotion, prayer, kindness at home, purity of deed and thought, counted nothing if the regular words of the ruling power were not pronounced. The most exemplary men, the tenderest mothers, the most gentle daughters, fathers whose families were dear to them beyond language, were hurried to the flames or rack because they could not say the words fixed upon by the pope or the tyrant in power. It was words, words, words, and death everywhere. No estimate was placed upon the inward life. Myriads died singing or praying to the spiritual God and their lives had been full of purity.

Elizabeth imprisoned for life all who conducted religious service without using her Prayer Book. Persons not believing in bishops were branded with an iron. Anabaptists and Arians were tortured and then hung. As internal piety was little dreamed of as being a religious test, it was as absent from man as from God. God was a being partial to a prayer-book or to a bishop. Forms were everything. Knox declared that one mass was more fearful to him than ten thousand armed enemies landed in any part of the realm, never harboring, for an instant, the idea that beneath the service of the mass there might be a pious heart. There was no weighing of soul; it was all a listening to words, and a crowding to the fagot those whose words deviated a hair's breadth from the model held in the hand of some bloated ruler or licentious priest. In this awful reign of iron sentences little girls of childhood innocence, and mothers whose love is an emblem to earth of love infinite, went down to early tombs in the double agony of flesh and heart; but the heart of a dove counted nothing in an age of vowels and consonants. Catholic words killed thousands of Protestants, and Protestant words killed thousands of Catholics.

All imaginable doctrines have, in the long, bloody period,

been made a ground of life or death. Words about baptism, words about the Trinity, words about the pope, words about transubstantiation, words about the Virgin Mary, words about the Eucharist, words about the doctrine of purgatory, about astronomy have exposed the body to the stake and the soul to perdition. The holiness of Galileo were of no avail if he taught that the earth turned round each day. It was not an inner belief that was demanded, but an outward unity of dogmas. Hence life was offered to heretics if they would only repeat the rejected dogma. What he really believed was not a matter of importance, if he uttered the conventional creed. No change of heart was expected or thought of, for the soul was not so much thought of as church unity. The outward othodoxy was the grand consideration. Hence when Galileo consented to the idea that the earth does not turn and that the sun does go around it, he descended from the public penitential platform saying in a whisper, "The earth moves." No one cared for his inner thought if he only stood by the public words on the subject.

This zeal for dogma resulted from two causes. First cause, the fact that man comes slowly to a spiritual religion. That is the perfection of worship, and hence like all perfection must come slowly and come last. To get away from the outward and to throw one's whole being into the idea that what God demands is a pure heart is a condition of mind to which only Christ and the angels have yet come.

A second cause of the enthronement of dogmas lay in the union of church and government. A new dogma might build up a new party, a new party might displace the party or power. The class believing the earth to turn around might become so powerful as to overthrow the party that plainly heard the Bible declare the sun to rise and set, and that saw the sun set every day. The inner life of a man was nothing, the silent belief of a philosopher was of no moment, but the perpetuity of the party in power, the long continuance of power and incomes was very desirable, and hence the dogmas held by the party on the throne must be spoken to the crowd by all, and by all constantly and everywhere. Certain assemblages of words stood for the pope. Other words might exalt an astronomer or a Pantheist and his followers. Thus forgiveness was always offered a victim even on the pile of fagots if he would repeat the pet ideas of the church, because the church meant not salvation, so much as power and regular incomes!

In our own country it has been the sorrow of us all to see a doctrine regarding slavery made more conspicuous, for a half century, than the doctrine of a pure life, rendered a test of orthodoxy not because of any heaven or hell, but because of Congress and patronage, and high and low caste. Thus in these two causes — the difficulty in the way of a spiritual religion and the identity of church and state one may find the influences that gave mankind a religion not of the soul, but of many and intricate, and often contemptible doctrines.

That there are great doctrines, the obedience of which is life, the disobedience of which is death, is very evident. Truth is the food of life, the stuff that life is made of; but these truths are few compared with that assemblage of ideas that can be seen on the bloody field of history. Each aspirant had a discrimination of idea upon which to base hope, not of heaven so much as of earth. Certain ideas stood not for a virtue, but for a party in the church or state. They were not paths of spiritual salvation, but the emblems of authority. Like the secret words of masonry, they were not words that converted a soul, but words that stood for an empire. Morgan was put to death not because the ideas he uttered were valuable, but because they had been agreed upon and stood for a masonic order. So heretics were burned, not because what they said interfered with virtue, but because it interfered with some mitre or crown. A new idea was treason. This was all done in the name of sincerity for it was easy for the Deity, who had once been a Deity of gifts, to become one of dogmas. God became a Being to be worshipped with dogmas. A man not baptized was so offensive to God that hell was only too good a place for that soul! An infant not baptized died hopeless, God was so partial to baptism! If this baptism were not administered by the proper church, it was still worse than no baptism, God was so partial to a particular church! And thus onward, until the blessed God was wholly occupied in the protection of a hundred forms of speech, and the human soul was occupied, not with purity of heart, but with repeating the terms pleasing to the ideal Deity and the pope. This pope was not always Catholic; sometimes he was Protestant.

Now salvation is a term whose meaning depends upon that which is lost. If one has lost property, his salvation will be the recovery of that property or its equivalent. If one has lost his good name by false accusation, his salvation will be found in the emblazonment of the falsehood, and on the return of public good will. This man does not need much dogma but rather, he needs acquittal and a better fame. If the soul has lost virtue and piety, then salvation will be found in a return to piety and purity, and the truths of salvation will be those that lead him to that one result. This is the destiny of Christ's mediation. Hence the essence of religion is found in the one event or phenomenon, a righteous heart. Gifts to the Deity were the infant creepings of religion, the shadow of a coming reality, the manifestations of an incipient love that did not know how to express itself. Not knowing that what God most wished was a pure heart in His children, they loaded His temples with their jewels and raiment, and His altars with their lambs.

Then came the days that brought God an offering of words. Imagining Him to be a God of articles and forms, they repeated thousands of words and baptized their guilty foreheads in much or little water as an act of salvation.

And now the world awaits the last transfiguration of human worship, into a spiritual condition, into a soul lifted above sin, and exulting in a nearness to the image of God. The nations await with tears of past sorrow, a religion that shall indeed baptize men and children, either or both, but counting this as only a beautiful form shall take the souls of men into the atmosphere of Jesus, and into the all-pervading presence of God, and detain them there, until sin shall have become a hated monster, and perfection of spirit the heaven of this life, and that to come. Terms must give place to righteousness and communion with God.

In our day the empire of words still lingers. The churches are still wedded to quantity more than to quality, but wedded by bonds that are growing weaker under the uprising of the "inner life" philosophy. The churches still eagerly keep count of their membership, and publish the members that joined their bodies last year, but keep no record of the number of Christians that lived dishonorable lives in the last decade, quantity rather than quality still being a ruling passion in our half-civilized world. But Jesus Christ was not gifts, nor words, nor quantity, but quality; and surely as the world shall last, mankind, under His leadership shall march nearer and nearer to the world of spirit, where quantity and words shall all be overwhelmed by the sweet music, "Blessed are the pure in heart."

If Christ was anything, He was spiritual perfection. He was not a voice saying "Lord, Lord," but He was a spotless soul. Hence the world coming up to His religion, at last, will find itself in an atmosphere not full of the tenets of Elizabeth, or Mary, or Calvin, but full of that transcendent whiteness that indicates that sin has been washed away and that the righteousness of Heaven has come to the heart, like a joyous morning in paradise.

In this coming era upon whose margin I do feel that the world is standing now, like Florida upon the border of flowery spring, our citizens, our fathers, our brothers, our friends, our children, will move before us, not with conventional words upon their lips, but with faces radiant with the consciousness of a nobler life. The good deeds of yesterday, the good deeds of to-day, the perfected goodness of the morrow, a deep love for man, a consciousness of the presence of God will fill the whole face with a nobleness and happiness to which earth has thus far been willingly a stranger. This will be a salvation and Christ will be a Saviour.

And as for those dear ones, who in the long past have died because of words, the Covenanter children, whose parents were burned before their eyes in fires of agony and orphanage; the Quakers, flying before the vengeance of outraged dogmas; the Catholics murdered because they looked toward Jesus through some symbol, will all come back to a spirit-shore, where Christ will know His children by the golden thread of love in their hearts and where no fallible human judgment can ever come to separate a Christian soul from the realm of perfect liberty, perfect justice, and perfect happiness. Man as a ruler, as a tyrant, has perished. He lives only as a brother. The dominion and power have returned to the Infinite One — infinite in tenderness.

THE VALUE OF YESTERDAY.*

David Swing.

For ask now of the days that are past. *Deuteronomy*, iv:32.

Time is one of the incomprehensible things. If we gaze up into the blue sky, and thus shut out all lowly objects, and then repeat the word time to our soul, we will find ourselves absorbed in a deep mystery. Each breath we take lies partly in the past, partly in the present, partly in the future. One of the most beautiful sentences uttered over the name of Jesus Christ is that one of Paul—"Christ, the same yesterday, to-day and forever.

Time divides itself into these three continents—yesterday, to-day, and to-morrow, each grand, and each peculiar—and each measureless. The divinity that presides over to-morrow is called Hope; the present has no guardian by name, and the divinity of yesterday is called Memory. There is no eloquence, no poetry, no process of reasoning that can do justice to the beauty and influence of any one of these periods. Looking backward and forward the heart becomes overwhelmed with the weight and mystery of the theme.

The study of the distances in the heavens in which we find that there are suns whose light could not have reached our world in less than a million years, is scarcely less bewildering than this contemplation of the yesterday and the to-morrow. Led by its own impulse the human heart has always prized the morrow more than the present, or the yesterday, and hence has written the most of its poetry in the name of Hope. Hope has always been the popular goddess of earth's children. When all other shrines are vacant, this one receives its daily offerings of flowers. When the seven classic philosophers were holding a banquet together, it was asked of them, "What is the most universal possession?" The reply agreed upon as most accurate was the word hope, for he that has nothing else has hope.

But this extreme popularity and worship of futurity constitute a reason why the mind should guard against a total oblivion of all else and form an excuse for reading before you this morning the words of the text, "Ask now the days that are past." For the hour let us oppose the orators and the poets and the

* A discourse delivered in McVicker's theatre, Sunday morning, June 1, 1873, by Prof. David Swing.

youth and beauty of the realm, and speak in behalf of yesterday. We shall not find the same loveliness of person that belongs to Hope, but what is wanting in bloom and smile may find compensation in wisdom and pensiveness.

The days that are past are like a mother whose youth and powers of mind and affections have all failed in the life-long devotion to her children. The marks in her forehead, the whiteness of her face, the solemnity of her heart are only proofs that her bloom and vivacity have journeyed over to her loved ones, and their life, their love, their works, their language, their song are a direct inheritance from the one who is soon to be recalled from their sight. Thus Yesterday, going back to the tomb of Solomon or Moses, or in that longer journey proposed by recent sciences is, whether we go back a thousand or a million years, the mother of us all, and the tomb, and ruins of all the nations are only marks upon the forehead of this great parent; they are the whiteness of that face which faded in behalf of new life and new happiness. The lonely silent pyramids, the brilliant ruins of the Acropolis, of Palmyra, of Thebes, the deeply entombed streets of old Jerusalem, all the ivy-covered minsters of Europe, Catholic or Protestant,are fragments of that home where Yesterday lived and taught the new generations playing about her feet.

The greatness of man as pictured in the future may be a dream so far as our life, or our nation's life is concerned, but the past is a great fact of which nothing can rob us,and whose worth no fancy can over-estimate. In order to behold the presence and kindness of God, it is not necessary to draw upon the powers of hope any more than upon the powers of memory. It is a confessed truth that by nature we look for the most and and highest good in the future, and, since God is the ideal of goodness, the soul beholds Him unveiling himself in days that are to come. We say, "Our Father in Heaven," more in anticipation of what He will be than in confession of what He has been; for the sin and suffering of earth make it logically necessary for us to select the future as the arena of the Creator. But, having confessed this logical superiority of the future, the past yet remains a vast field of religious truth and sentiment.

Let it be granted that there is a personal God whom we define as the sum of all perfections, yet we could not prove that it was necessary that this God should have expressed all His attributes in the very first years of human life. If it was lawful for the human race to begin in a childhood that could neither speak nor walk, and if it was lawful for all science and art to begin with simple lessons and slowly work forward, it would seem equally lawful that the Creator should not unfold all His glory to the first generation, but should strew it along for a ten thousand or million years period. All the beauties of earth are progressive beauties, all the arts are progressive arts, all the sciences are progressive sciences—and hence one might expect that the infinite love of God would be subject to a slow manifestation of itself. A *priori* reason would suppose, perhaps, that a God of love would be found proceeding as such from the outset in the history of a creature like man, and that man would never know a year or a moment of sin or pain, that barbarism and depravity would be impossible for a day or an hour. But being driven by the facts away from the use of a *priori* logic we must fall back to the second best logic, and, following the phenomena of science and art and all human activity, must suppose that God selects not a day or a year for His own full emblazonment, but a vast epoch such as is demanded by geology or the study of the stars. With this confession in our minds we can "ask now the days that are past," and see in man's face and language and laws and arts the gradual unfolding of divine wisdom and love.

A child taken from our public schools at the age of twelve years and examined in reading, in conversation, in knowledge, in music, will be found to possess a language that consumed six thousand years in its construction; it will be found to possess knowledge that has been wrought out by the toil and perhaps sorrow of a hundred generations. It will sing perhaps a song, "My Country 'tis of Thee, or "Home Sweet Home," that is the upshot of thousands of years of sentiment and thought about liberty and home. What then is a bright pure school child to-day, but a place where God's love and wisdom in days that are past have treasured up their tenderness as the earth treasures up the dust that for millions of years has filtered down upon it out of the invisible either in which the worlds all float?

But pass from the school child to all the school children, and to all the adult minds and hearts that move upon the earth, listen to all their wisdom and music and industry and eloquence, and do you not feel that this multitude measures a great revelation of God above that day when earth possessed but one man or family, and that one without language and without learning and without virtue?

There are two theories about the origin of man. The one that he was made in his present form by the Creator by a simple instantaneous command, the other that man is the result of a long development and mutation of species. Thus the only dreamed of theories give us only one human being in the outset, and that one a human being defective in language, in art,in learning, in hope, in memory. Defective in language because there was nothing to be said; in art for there was no one to admire the skill; in learning because there was no language in which to express facts; in hope because there was no realization of any imperfection or death; in memory because there was nothing to be remembered.

In the first human being therefore, God could no more display His perfections than a musician like Mozart could unfold his genius to an infant, or to a South Sea Islander. Could the divine virtue be perceived by a being that had not perceived sin? Could the divine immortality be appreciated by an individual who was a stranger to death? Could the divine omniscience be felt by a being that had not yet learned or developed the love of knowledge? By no means. Could the sun reveal its power and beauty if it had nothing but a clod to shine upon? Give it a planitary system, skies, stars, clouds, continents, seas, fruits, flowers, and it possesses then an arena for its play of color and light.

In order that God should reveal himself, a race was necessary, not only moving in vast multitudes, but moving along vast periods of time; and hence, recalling the days that are past, the heart in the least religious may perceive a Creator scattering the attributes and truths of His own being.

You tell me God is sinless. Looking into the future we perceive only a dream, and turn away uncertain, but, looking into that vast realm called Yesterday,and perceiving that sin has always brought sorrow, and that virtue has brought beauty of face, and life and peace of heart, I come back from that survey feeling that righteousness is a divine attribute. The sins of men are so inwoven with the sorrows of men that this very tumult and perpetual weeping are only an announcement of the benediction, "Blessed are the pure in heart, for they shall see God." But it is impossible to descend to particulars. We can only say that the immense past of humanity may be viewed as a field in which the arts and the industries and the philosophies and religion, taking the form at last of Christianity, have gradually found opportunity for the revelation of their glorious natures.

But, turning aside from thoughts about God's own emblazonry, think of man himself and his immediate personal relation to the days that are past. As we said in the outset, great is the office of hope. We have no word too good or extreme for that faculty, but we would enter a plea in behalf of the value of yesterday in its relations to mind and heart. Hope is a grand sentiment, but it conveys no information. All the information of the soul comes up from the days that are gone. Hence one of the best thinkers said, "Not to know history is to be always a child." The value of the ideas that enter into human life is chiefly to be learned by watching their evolution and workings in that great workshop called Yesterday. Take the idea of liberty, and no dreamer who looks into the future can behold its length and breadth, but he alone can measure the import of the term who hears the cry of the slave from the days of the Romans down to the career of our own land, and who sees the prosperity of freedom from Athens to Florence, and from Florence to England and America. Take the idea of home, and if you would feel the import of the word, look not forward into poetic haze, but back into human experience, in the tears of sadness and joy that have fallen by the feet of any exile going away or coming back; or look into your own childhood and consult its memories and then the term unveils itself with no light or shadow left out.

Beyond the unfolding of truths Yesterday possesses another power—that of softening and modulating the mind and heart. Egotism draws its vanity from a perfect forgetfulness of yesterday. Self-consciousness and coming greatness erase all else from the mind, and the egotist stands great in his possibilities. He is just about to conquer a world or greatly surprise one. Any deep study of his own or of the world's yesterday would drain his heart of the last drop of personal vanity, for there was an arena and he did not conquer nor astonish a world—and there all those who were more highly endowed are sleeping in forgotten dust. If the past utters anything that is of value it is that all self-worship and glorification are the weakest shape human nature can assume, and that there is nothing worth living for except the general mental and moral progress of self and of mankind. The great graves are those which cover the dust of hearts that did some work that entered after them into the public welfare and happiness.

There is no vanity away from man. The sea gives us her music without egotism. The rainbow spreads out her gorgeous lines without boasting. The nightingale sings her notes herself unseen among the wild thorn, in the silent night. The floral world in June fills the air with perfume, and the sight with her indescribable tints, but without any ostentation. Man alone has vanity; not because man alone has soul for this would be to degrade soul below the standard of dumb life; but because man alone has wandered from the divine path. This wandering has been aided and abetted by his blindness to yesterday, and by living only in the proud thrones and crowns and glories of to-morrow. Vanity draws its chief nutriment from the future. This is, perhaps, the reason why nearly all of us pass through a vain period in early years. Fortunate is the heart that did not, in early life, pass through a score of years of personal greatness. The animal spirits and poetry of youth make it despise the past, and dwell only in the land of hope, and as the future contains nothing that can humiliate, contains no tombs, no disappointment, no dust of the heart, it carries the young soul away from truth and decorates it in its own regal and gaudy drapery. But when the past begins to be recognized by the mind, when the soul looks back at its own path and the great path of mankind, a spirit rises from that wide, silent ocean that drives away all self-worship and makes man stand up in a combined strength and humility—the only combination worthy of man or his Maker.

It may, perhaps,be a beautiful providence that young persons look only into the future, for there certainly should be some years of life set apart for a happiness without much alloy—and such a joy does come from a steady gaze toward that realm whose gates are not only always garlanded ; but are always open. But if this be so, then I know there is another providence also that makes man as he draws near the noontime of life, labor and usefulness, begin to look back and find in the history of man a sober truth and a self-forgetfulness and love of mankind which the rosy future could not give. Hence despise not the years when you find your reflection begins to look back, for God has not without reason placed behind the human race a long five or ten thousand years, and it is not without reason that this past is constantly becoming more immense and more varied. It is the soil out of which man grows and is to grow, and the longer the rains wash down the mountain sides, and the more of yesterday's leaves and grasses mingle with the mold, the greater will be the productions of to-morrow.

Yesterday contains all the battlefields in which freedom was gradually wrought out from many threads all dipped in blood. Yesterday contains the experiment and the failure of all despotisms. Yesterday con tains the onset and defeat of every form of sin and vice. Yesterday holds the ashes of all beauty, and of all life except that of the soul with God. Yesterday is full of past usefulness and of its ways and means, full of tears and their causes and cures. In that shadowy domain there stands the cross, and there is the Saviour dying for the vast myriads of a race. God has not without reason thrown such an immense history behind His children of to-day. It must be that out of the world that has been there is always flowing down to those who are living a stream of wisdom and character that bears onward to a sacred destiny.

The past is the long, uniform trade-wind that bears the spirit along toward its far off haven. The ship striking those winds has around it a friend that shall for days and nights and for weeks, without calm or storm, bear it along over the wide sea. The human spirit, if it will guide its course properly, may pass into such a moving air, that, without storm or calm, will day and night throw it along toward a better,nobler home.

The poet Dryden bequeathed us a poem upon this great dream of to-morrow:

> Trust on and think the morrow will repay,
> The morrow's falser than the former day;
> Lies worse, and while it says you shall be blest,
> Steals all the pleasures that you once possessed.

Aware of the value and beauty of hope, and not daring to depreciate it in the least,yet I do wish you all to feel that there are two other powerful influences in human life,in each individual life, to-day and yesterday. A bad yesterday is the saddest condition of the soul. If one can only look back upon a good yesterday, the future need not be feared; but if yesterday was marked by a great crime or folly I do not see how there could be an eternity long enough or purifying enough to wash it white. There may be some river Lethe known only to God and created by His mercy, dipped into which the soul may forget its vice and crime, but reason looking upon the Catherines de Medici, or upon the violent murderers of our own land, cannot see anything in the countless years of eternity that could erase the vision and memory of the black spot. "Things past," Livy says," may be repented of, but never erased." Yesterday is nothing but to-day passed over by our mind and heart. The great duty of the hour is, not to gaze with poetic rapture into the future, but to weave out of the present a glorious past.

One of our poets says: "To-morrow do thy worst for I have lived to-day." And the old Martial says: "Didst thou say thou wilt live to-morrow? He is the wise man who lived yesterday." To-day is the sublime part of life because it is continually making that yesterday which will always follow us go where we may in this life or one to come. Aristotle says there is one thing which God cannot change and that is yesterday. If this is so and we all feel that it is, then there is one thing better than all high resolve—namely noble deeds already done. Better therefore than hope of great things to come is the memory of good already performed. Shakspeare says:

> "To-morrow and to-morrow and to-morrow,
> Creeps in this petty pace from day to day
> To the last syllable of recorded time;
> And all our yesterdays have only lighted fools
> The way to dusty death."

Oh my friends before whose feet the stream of life is running sweetly to-day, and above all oh ye young hearts who have as yet no yesterday, but in whose hands its destiny is lying all untouched and ready to be formed for joy or grief—do not despise to-day, and fill your eyes with only the vision of glittering hope; do not sit upon the banks of this stream waiting for its waters to run by and bring you the beautiful future, but pour out your heart's powers and life upon the present, because it is creating a Yesterday whose smile, if it wears one, will never perish, and whose tears of sin, if it has them, not even a merciful God can wipe away.

The chief part of your life is not that which spreads out before you, but it will soon be that which shall lie back of you. The impulse of a river is not in the broad expanse where it emerges into the sea, but is far back of that in the table lands and mountain ranges of a vast continent, all which, having caught the rains and having dissolved the snows of yesterday crowd the stream forward in a majestic sweep. The wide mouth of the Amazon is the result of the storms and snows of a thousand winters. Thus life should not go on allured only by poetic hope, but pressed forward by the momentum and majestic flow of days that are gone. Heaven is a height to which men climb on the deeds of this life. Hence the Bible speaking of the dead coming to heaven, says: "Their works do follow them." Oh yes, these works make the soul; they weave its life out of their golden threads; they fill it with wisdom and love and humility, and then throw it forward to heaven as the south wind carries northward in spring the song of birds and the garlands of flowers. Hope is herself founded upon the past. It is a glorious past only that produces a serene, glorious hope. Yesterday is the foundation of the Heavenly City. Hope is the sweet blue sky in which the structure rises. Oh friends, combine both hope and memory. Coming to the grave he only can look forward with joy who can sweetly look back.

VARIATION OF MORAL MOTIVE.*

DAVID SWING.

The love of Christ constraineth us.— *Corinthians v. : 13.* Love is the fulfilling of the law.— *Romans xiii. : 10.*

The world is so vast that no human foot can travel over it, and no heart occupy all places with its home. Going to Florida in winter, or Switzerland in the summer months, or to the New England hills in autumn, one feels that in each of these wonderful kingdoms of nature, he should build his home, and live his whole life. Coming to the borders of a sweet lake in our own Northwest, looking down from a silent forest into the waters that are clear as glass to the depth of hundreds of feet, the heart suddenly feels that it is good to be there, and wishes to build three tabernacles for self and friends, upon the spot where such divine beauty seems transfigured. We forget our limits of space and enjoy a feeling of infinity of space and of perpetual life.

Then the thought comes that one cannot live every where. Do all we may there will be beautiful spots where we can possess no house. There will be waters we cannot look into, bird songs we may not hear. It is sorrowful that there are seas whose waves do not beat for us. Building by the lakes a voice comes up from the Mexican gulf inviting us to its early spring. Building by a mountain solitude the city sends out to us its joyous shout, its music, its art, its eloquence—and the mountain home is tempted even to ruin by a counter charm. Sad warfare between finite man and infinite beauty!

In this bewilderment of the beautiful there is no alternative left the heart but to conclude that the world is too large for it. It cannot go all over it, cannot hold it all in its arms. Life is too short for the enjoyment of all the grand days that open their morning portals between the St. Lawrence and the Amazon, between the Black Sea and the Golden Gate. There is a tomb in the grass that cuts short this wandering from joy to

* A discourse delivered at Standard Hall, Sunday morning, June 23, 1872, by Prof. David Swing.

joy. The tomb is the author of all eclectism. With traces of sorrow perhaps, but with resignation, the limited mortal heart must say, the world is too large for me, and must select its spot for life and for death. It must plant a few vines and trees and make the most of its narrow realm. We cannot pluck all roses, the hand being made for but one.

So the moral world of our God is too large. It outreaches our mind and affections. It hath motives too many for any one, but just enough for all; too many for a life, but enough for all lives. All mankind make up a kind of infinity of mind and heart, and an eternity of time, and in this vast sea of humanity all God's moral beauties and forces find demand. But in any one soul fluttering along over only a few years, as a winged butterfly flits only over one summer's foliage, the divine motives cannot all find full field of action. The heart not being able to live every where must contentedly pitch its tent in some vale, and say, "Here will I live and die." We would not narrow down life from choice, but accept the order of necessity. We would struggle to grasp as much as possible, but with the full assurance that to comprehend and enjoy all is denied us in God's decree.

The text, embody one of the fragments of the great realm of motive. Christ's love of man and man's love of Christ, cause and effect, make up a grand incentive to virtuous action. These are not the whole of truth. They are golden branches plucked from a great tropical wilderness. For the love of Christ is not the only thing that restrains, nor is love the only fulfilment of the law. In Oriental language a part is a whole, and one beautiful thing is a complete world. The fear of punishment also restrains. The fear of Christ restrains, and love is often found in great depth and yet the law is not fulfilled. Paul had just said, "Knowing the terror of the Lord we persuade men," and, "We must all appear before the judgment seat of Christ." Such souls as Peter had, loved deeply, and yet had fallen into sin; so that love did not fulfil the law. The "terror of the Lord" was invoked to help restrain, and yet, amid these phenomena come the words, "Love is the fulfilment of the law" and "The love of Christ constraineth us." Beautiful transformation of what we love into a whole universe.

The philanthropic leaders in our age are wonderfully constrained by the love of mankind. Pity for the poor human race, daily moves the best hearts that have ever lived. Before this immense influence hundreds of our best men bow as before a divine command. Thus we perceive that the world of moral motives is as rich as the world of physical beauty, and if a single heart cannot build its home by every beautiful vale, but must go from the many to the one; so, in the world of morals, the heart cannot but retreat from the whole universe, to take refuge in a part. Its house must be by this river or lake, but not by all waters that sleep or run. The love of Christ is a beautiful part of the moral world. It is stated as if a universe; but this is a statement of love, rather than of logic. Love always confuses its dream with the picture of infinity. "Love is the fulfilling of the law," is also a sublime part of the moral world. It is quoted as being the whole, but this too, is the language of admiration rather than of logic; for if this were the whole truth, it would only be necessary for men to be sincere in sentiment, and their love would be the same as perfection. In the midst of a universe so vast, what can the poor limited heart do, but accept of some one great impulse an impulse acquired by taste, by locality, or by inheritance, and build there its earthly house for it's few years here below?

There is a sect of Christians now rising up in our land, or rather coming into the world a second time, who have reached what they call the higher life. Led by such noble minds as Professor Upham and Dr. Boardman, and Inskip, they have developed a piety, which has eliminated, not only all doubt from their mind, but all care and sorrow from their heart. To them no pain can come. They are glad when their friends die, for they see heaven so near, and they say that God is so with them, that this earth is a border of Paradise. They have reproduced with additional beauties the quietism of Madame Guyon of the seventeenth century. Turning their gaze upon only peace in God it has become a universe and all else has faded from their horizon.

Thus in tranquility of soul there is found a motive of life, a power that hurls into the sea of oblivion the sin that comes from this world's temptation, and the sorrow that comes from its physical pain and death. The grave is the cradle from which earth turns away and leaves the sleeping child to be rocked of angels and to awake with God. These fresh hearts may be in error to-day, as that woman and the great Fenelon were two hundred years ago; but they illustrate the general fact, that one or two motives are all that the heart can carry, and these become to that heart a whole world. They are to it immensity and eternity.

To the city of God there are many paths, paths for different centuries, different meridians, and different individuals. There was something in the times of Calvin and Luther and on to Jonathan Edwards, that enabled the motive of punishment to be very influential for good. To inquire whether anything would have done as good service, would be about like the inquiry, whether some other method of light and heat might not have been resorted to by the Creator, that would have made our existing sun unnecessary. It is certain that "the terror of the Lord" wielded a mighty influence on the past centuries; and the same impulse of virtue will always be extant and active; but to the millions of a subsequent age a new impulse is liable to arise, and, expressing itself in the words, "the love of Christ constraineth us," may, for a time, be a complete universe to the existing heart. The horizon is daily swept for new clouds.

New motives are always unfolding and blossoming with new colors. Our fullest roses were once single leafed. Some seek riches for fear of a poor-house at last, or the jail for debt. Nobler minds seek wealth, because of the education and beauty it will buy for the dear loved ones, or for the brothers in the street. Each age and each form of government is fashioning a religious argument for itself, despotism admitting the element of authority, republicanism admitting the sweeter influence of good result, caring less for *ipse dixit* than for the fitness of things. Motives come and go along with the coming and going of new times and new men. The arguments for a holy life change. The old ones do not become false, but they fail to please. New ones are demanded by the new minds and hearts coming into life. In the childhood of you in this hall, who are oldest to-day, it was customary to frighten young hearts into virtue. We little children feared a dark room for reasons good then, but poor now. All misfortunes were the vengeance of our Heavenly Father following some bad act of the past week or day. We did not hear much about the text, "Whom the Lord loveth He chasteneth." But the Christian children of to-day, are led along virtue's path, by being shown the lovely side of Christianity. Music, books, Christmas festivals, tender Sabbath-school teachers and a thousand inventions of love, draw their spirits up toward that Being, who gave existence and name to Christianity. The new motive rises like a star. The love of Christ constrains them.

There can be no one impulse to virtue that shall monopolize all souls and all times. Mind is too full of variety. The times change too much and we are too much changed in them. If there be one word deeply carved upon God's works that word is *variation.* In the strata of the earth, on its surface, in the faces of men, in the pursuits of society there is the record of a God who is infinite in forms and qualities. Next to the beauty of God's unchangeableness in principles, comes the beauty of His variety in non-essentials The laws of vegetation are perpetual, but the leaves and flowers and fruits vary. The peach was born yesterday, but trees, in the eternity past. God is fixed as to righteousness for himself and for His children; but the motives to it among men assume new shapes with the shifting time and place. It is always purity that lies before the soul; but whether the heart shall be led to it by the intrinsic goodness of the object or by the fear of punishment for seeking the opposite are details that admit of variation. A deliberative mind will be influenced by both ideas the passionate heart by only the goodness of virtue, seeking it as the hungry child seeks food; the cowardly, timid nature will seek it from fear. The variety of motive will be demanded by the variety of mind.

A deeply religious woman objects to the hymn,

" Prone to wander Lord I feel it
Prone to leave the God I love,"

saying that she feels no proneness to wander none to leave the God she loves. She says, " How would it sound in our ear for a mother to sing to her child,

'Prone to wander child I feel it
Prone to leave the child I love' "?

To a nature of this kind the motives of Christian life are formed on Christ himself. All considerations of perdition are out of the question. The love of Christ constraineth. Love is the fulfilling of law in all this passionate heart. It was so in the school of Madame Guyon and Fenelon and the Wesleys—and will always be so whenever the soul rises to a passion in love and faith. Perfect love casteth out fear.

The higher life of religion will find its motive in religion itself. As the musician finds his motive, not in the pain of discord, but in the sweetness of music, so the higher order of Christian life will find its impulse, not in any fear of hell, but in the beauty and good of Jesus Christ. As art is not the avoidance of deformity, but the study of positive beauty, so Christianity is not a flight from wrath, but a loving development and enjoyment of the more perfect life. God is not to be sought because there is a Satan, but because there is a God.

When patriotism runs low and there is impending war it is necessary for the State to repeat the law that treason is death. This law is a perpetual fact. This law will never be repealed, but it is kept in existence only by the low form of patriotism possible here and there. But the true citizen lives above it, and ignores it, and wholly forgets it, for his positive love of his native land constrains him. It fulfils the law. Behind the mercenary Persian troops went the driver with his whip, a man with a whip behind each squad, and the victory came not from love of country, but from fear of the scourge; but the moment a country becomes worthy of love and its citizens become intelligent enough to love it, the whip behind the soldiers is superceded by the honor and happiness in front. The flag overhead with its red, white and blue carries a divine impulse in its waving folds. Its threads are the threads of life—its red is the blood of men's hearts. Before this banner of beauty the fear of a Persian whip falls out of all use and even remembrance.

It would be dreadful if Christianity were less noble than patriotism and must be expected to draw its activity from a whip on the field of battle. The banner of salvation is grander than any that ever waved over bloody fields, even of human liberty. It rustles in the winds of immortality. It is not the flag of a transient state full of the graves of our children, but the flag of that great Fatherland where there is no death and no tears. Under its snowy white and its heavenly azure soldiers in the higher life need no impulse but the love of their passion-full hearts.

Hence the better men become, the more Christ-like Christians become; the more will the world of punishment give place to the world ot peace and joy in the presence of Jesus Christ, and the more intelligent and cultivated men become, the more will they be moved by the positive side of religion; by its excellence rather than by its penalties.

But amid all the fluctuations of patriotism the law of death for treason remains written on the statute book of nations. And so in Christianity however any class or any age may rise above the influence of penalty for sin, yet punishment remains a perpetual fact in the ecomony of our God. Its dark cloud will rise or fall according to the quality of humanity. Wherever there are hearts that can see no goodness in holiness, none in honesty, and in charity, none in Jesus Christ, none in the worship of God, wherever there are minds incapable of being led by the intrinsic good of religion, there this dark cloud of divine wrath is ready to descend and to envelop with its thunders the soul that cannot and will not be enveloped by love. The result of sin expressed in all religions by the word "hell" is a perpetual influence, liable to go and come as humanity advances or retreats in the path of intelligence and morals,—but it must be a perpetual fact in a world of beings capable of being immoral. A world of sin must be a world of penalty.

As we said in the outset one heart cannot live in all the beautiful places of earth, neither can it be led by all the motives of entire humanity. What is true of a mind may be true of an age. It is possible for a whole age to become like Guyon and Fenelon, enamored of one idea, and, forgetting the gloomy hell, draw all its spiritual life from a vision of Jesus Christ and of His redeemed earth and happy paradise. The love of Christ may constrain a whole age. This ought particularly to become the case in an age of unusual education and culture, and in an age that develops the goodness ana benevolence of Jesus Christ. An age that loves the poor, that feeds and clothes the destitute and famine stricken, that pours out millions upon a burned up city. that governs its children by love instead of torture, that enthrones kindness in public schools and even in prisons and jails, and that does all these new things in the name of a positive study of Christ, will not be an age that will constantly threaten mankind, but an age that will gently lead men toward the divine Jesus of Nazareth.

In days when men cannot whip their children, in days when men are arrested for cruelty to dumb beasts, in days when we teach our children beautiful hymns and when we reward them for any act of goodness, in days when there are homes for the friendless and for the fallen, and millions are poured out for colleges where anybody can learn any science or art without charge, in days when a child need not be a beggar, in days in which Russia and America are fresh in the glory wreaths of having set free 60,000,000 of slaves it can hardly be expected that the pulpit, ignoring this grand uprising of tenderness, will daily point the horrors of perdition while the very street is being enchanted by this vision of love. Oh what a betrayal this would be of the pulpit's trust!

It must be confessed that the motive of virtue found in the word punishment exists. It will always exist; but if there comes along an era that is blinded to this argument by having its eyes fixed upon the love of God and the Saviour, then let the public heart enjoy to the full this new, and powerful passion.

The terrors of the law have had whole periods allotted to themselves and they produced the middle ages, and before them, the Mosaic age. It is possible that an era that shall study the positive side of religion and shall fly to Christ, not because there is a Satan, but because there is a Christ, may work out for the human race better things than came from the age of monastic scourgings or from the penalties of Moses. A book loved under the name of "The New Testament" declares that "ye are not come unto a mount that might be touched and that burned with fire, nor unto blackness and darkness and tempest * * * * so terrible that Moses said 'I exceedingly quake and fear,' but ye are come unto Mount Sion and unto the city of the living God." The words spoken indeed to Christians do nevertheless announce to all mankind the ruling passion of the Gospel. Its great spectacle is not a Sinai but a Mount Sion, not a fiend devouring men, but a Saviour and a heavenly Father reaching out the open arms of infinite love to gather in us children.

If we have come to an age that seems to take up this dominant impulse of Christianity and to depress other motives we cannot but bless God that He postponed all our cradles and graves for this era of faith and love and peace. We are, I trust, all more than willing to give our hearts to the spirit of our own times, and would not for any gold go back to the age of terrorism in politics, in domestic life and in Christianity. Confessing punishment to exist as a potential idea, confessing prisons to exist for criminals, and death to threaten all traitors, and divine justice to hang like a cloud over sin, yet we must rejoice in all tendencies of ages and of men to base their moral life upon the attractiveness of the good.

A French writer living in the time of Louis XIV says: "Bourdaloue in his sermons astounds me." This was enough for one tongue. 'Massilon frightens me." That also was well. "Bossuet makes me believe." "Fenelon makes me to hope and love." Oh beautiful power of each of this matchless group! If individuals thus have a channel in which their souls must run all their life if it would go with any power or any happiness, so a whole generation may have its path, not as wide as all truth, but very beautiful to it and leading straight to paradise.

The preaching of religion from the standpoint of fear is the shortest mode, is the easiest method, if quantity of thought is considered, for it is only necessary to breathe familiar anathemas over all the sinful race of men. It is a longer and more difficult work to trace out the application of the Gospel to all the details of human life — to politics, to home, to childhood, middle life and old age. To gather up the rationalism of Christianity, its spiritualism — and its humanity, to unfold its Jesus Christ — its Holy Spirit, its faith, hope and charity — to develop in infinite riches of thought and feeling, is a hard, long task compared with the authoritative announcement of infinite sorrow to almost the whole human race. But let us all rejoice that the age demands of us all, pulpit and pew, the longer and more thoughtful method of proclaiming the manifold riches of Christianity.

The love of Christ that constrains us is not only a passion of that divine heart, but it is a wisdom and kindness penetrating a philosophy. This love of man flows and reflows through all the doctrines and precepts of the Gospel. In the golden rule, in the blessing of children, in the law of liberty and equality, in the doctrines of salvation, faith, penitence and purity, in the vision of God as a Father, in the delineation of immortal life, the love of Christ is perceived — like a beautiful soul inhabiting a beautiful body. It constrains us. It is not a simple passion of Christ for man, but it is a wisdom, an adaptation so kind that men call it love,— it being too full of warmth and tears to be called a philosophy.

CHRISTIANITY A LIFE.*

DAVID SWING.

" For the law of the spirit of life in Christ hath made me free from the law of sin and death."—*Rom. viii: 2.*

In the verses adjoining our text, Paul clothes the sinful nature of man with the attributes of a person or spirit, and thus while in man's intellect there is a spirit of good, there is in his body at large a spirit of evil. Instead of teaching the Manichæan idea of two souls, he seems only using the varied forms of illustration admissible in rhetoric, and in this liberty speaks of a good in the mind and an evil in the flesh. From this figure he passes to that of two laws, one that is spiritual, and one that is material, of the flesh, and when he would do good at the command of the former, he suddenly does bad at the command of the latter. As in a dream one often in his whole mind wishes to fly from danger but finds his feet unable to run or his voice to sound the alarm, and thus is wholly baffled by the conflict between his wishes and his feet, so Paul stood still, his life being neutralized between the conception of a noble life which lay in his reason and the instinct of a wicked life that lay in his flesh. He delighted in the law of God, but he saw another law in the members warring against the law of his mind, and bringing him into a captivity, and thus, oh wretched man that he was, with no one to deliver him from a body full of death, from a flesh that warred with the spirit. Thus might a dreamer, whose feet would not move in the moment of peril, pray to be set free from such a body of death that the released soul might escape. Commentators inform us that prisoners were often fastened to a dead body as part of their punishment; but evidently here Paul would love to be delivered from his own flesh, which carried in it such perpetual discord as to the spirit's highest ideal. He had a dead body of his own. While Paul was thus dragged in two ways by two equally balanced forces, there came to him a new force, even Christ, who turns the tide of battle, and soon the triumphant apostle said that the spirit of life in Christ had made him free from the law of sin and death. The influence of a life in Christ was so spiritual that the law of the humble, depraved flesh had retired from the strife, and had left the law of the mind free.

*Sermon delivered in Fourth Presbyterian Church, March 22, 1874.

From these seventh and eighth chapters springs up much of the "holiness" idea of some of the Methodists, and from them sprang the German mysticism of the fourteenth century; but to us living in a less impassioned age comes the plain lesson that Christianity is a Life. That spirit of life which was in Christ, that spirit of being, so far above the sins and wickedness of common humanity, developed also those who were "in Christ," and they walked no more after the flesh, but after the spirit. By common consent, if not by actual demonstration, it is affirmed of material things that they will perish. From the great gardens of Babylon to the hut of the peasant, from the splendor of marble palaces to the blooming roses, all, all, the the cheek of youth, the eye of beauty, will fade and become dust. So perfect is this desolation, that even the heavens must pass away as a scroll and the elements all melt with fervent heat. Along with this perishable organic world will go all the mental actions and emotions that were based wholly upon it. Appetite, passion, ambition, all states of mind that grew up from the material of earth, point downward toward that dust whence they came, and as the poet says,

"Here the sword and sceptre rust,"

along with them will perish the passion that drew the sword or the tyranny that swayed the sceptre.

On the other hand, by common consent, the world accepts of a spiritual realm which is the antithesis of the great dust-seeking kingdom, a world where all the ideas and sentiments and actions are tending away from the grave, and are reaching up toward where God dwells, to the land of immortal life. Love, charity, friendship, righteousness, benevolence, belong to a certain upper life called the life of the spirit.

Passing by the inquiry how the humble, dust-loving soul may be transformed into such a spiritual character as that one which came to Paul at Damascus, we come to the simple idea of the text that Christianity is a spiritual life as compared with a material or fleshly life; that it is a life regulated by a law of the spiritual world, the opposite of a life regulated by the law of sin and death.

When some of the former centuries came up to these two lives, the one of spirit and the other of flesh, they came to a great truth, but they ruined the great principles by their false definition of both the lives. They made the whole circle of human joy and industry and pleasure to be the life of sin and death, and they made a life of retirement and self-denial to be the ideal of spiritual existence. Hence came all that development of human sorrow seen in the old monastic, ascetic system. When we remember Pascal, who tried to eat his food without being conscious of its pleasant taste, and who would not permit his sister to address him kindly, lest he might experience the weakness of a human friendship; and when we read that a'-Kempis did not look upon the glory of springtime, because such material beauty might make him forget the moral beauty of God, we perceive the doctrine of a sinful and a higher life all ruined by the false definitions of the two shapes of being. They grasped the truth that religion is a life, but failed to know what life is in its truest significance. They thought the whole outer world a sin and a dungeon, the only arena of virtue. Our century having reached a new measurement of life, having defined the word "flesh" to mean only sinful pursuits, and having enlarged the spiritual life until it embraces all the pleasures and honors, all the faculties of body and soul, having reversed the past by declaring all God's world to be the arena of virtue, and a monk's cell to be the soul's eclipse, it should now come up afresh to the proposition that Christianity is a Life and by its new wisdom restore a truth which the past has already ruined by its folly. Before mankind will consent that Christianity is to be their life, they will need to know what you mean by "life," for if you indicate by that term the asceticism of Pascal, or the narrowness and severity of the Puritans, they will reject the religion as rapidly as all the pulpits can offer it. Only in the current year has a pamplet been issued by a clergyman, calling the attention of this synod to the alarming fact, that there are Churches all through the land in which have been built a kitchen department, and do in many ways thus dare to combine the temporal and the eternal. And last week we read a printed letter from some religionist, who was arguing with great zeal against the common household games of every kind, as being only stepping stones to the great games played for a stake. With such intellects ("If shape that can be called which shape hath none") to throw down before a community not naturally partial to the Gospel a definition of life, is to cast before the pulpit not only the common obstacle of original sin, but the additional stumbling-block of fresh, monkish absurdity. But for generations the Gospel has had to contend, not only against the "total depravity" of the world, but against the almost "total infirmity" of the Christian intellect, for, with the New Testament declaring Christ to be a life, the Church has almost drowned the voice by so defining "life," that educated persons could, with great difficulty, be persuaded to seek or even to admire it. With life defined as a solemnity, as a sorrow, with home transformed into a prison, of which the father was the jailer, with the Church conducted as a penance, with all the pleasures of life identified with sin, laughter being a form of evil spirit in the young, with Sunday weighed down by austerities, the Church, instead of making men free from the law of sin and death, rather perfected the bondage, and brought, if not sin, at least a death of the intellect and the heart.

Before we can preach Christ as a "new life," a life of the spirit, it is necessary that we declare before all the world that the spiritual life is wide and deep and beautiful. It is not the life of Pascal nor St. Bernard. It is not the life of the early Calvinist. It is not the life of the later Puritan, nor of the Quaker who despises music and literature, not of the pietists who have discarded reason, and who wait for the Holy Spirit to tell them when to sleep and when to wake, when to read and when to walk! No! Life must be defined with the map of earth before us, and into its pleasures must enter all the landscapes and all the seasons, all the fruits and flowers, all its forests, plains, and mountains; must be defined with the map of the mind before us, with all its faculties of conscience and reason and imagination and sentiment; must be defined with the map of society before us, with all the obligations and duties which spring from the presence of our fellow-men in all their conditions and destinies, and above all must be defined with the outlook of the soul before us, with its wonderful, almost divine, relations to God and the Savior, and to worship here and eternity hereafter. That it has called the infinite career of man as to this world by the name of "flesh," and has frowned upon it as being subject to the law of sin and death, is a calamity out of which our generation is struggling hard to escape, that it may find a religion which the young may accept without chilling their hearts, and which the educated may accept without exchanging a broad world of study for the narrowness and complainings of a monk.

Our century perceives that under all the pursuits and pleasures of this existence the law of a spiritual nature may lie, and that a naturalist, or a statesman, or a queen, or a musician, or a judge on the bench, or a young heart in the open fields, may be wholly within the spiritual life introduced to our gaze by the Savior. The law of the spirit of life in Christ is nothing more than a grand, broad human life, all pervaded by righteousness, and a certain elevated sentiment toward God and man. A spiritual life is only a life purified and elevated. It is not an existence *narrowed* as our ancestors thought, but a life sweetened by holier impulses. Compare the politics of Charles Sumner and the politics of Henry VIII. Under that of the American lay a spiritual law, lifting all his words up into the higher air of God; under that of the English king lay the law of the flesh, dragging the throne down toward the infernal world. Thus all through human being spirituality is not a shrinkage of the heart into the limits of a cell, but a purification of its vast natural breadth and depth. The middle age Christianity was a destruction of man, but the true Christianity is an expansion of the whole human intellect and sentiment. As the philosophy of Guizot or Cousin was only expanded by their spirituality above the philosophy of Epicurus, who said, "Let us eat, drink and be merry, for to-morrow we die," so all human life, from its love of nature and love of friends and love of truth, to all its powers of progress and enjoyment, is only enlarged by the spirituality which Christianity casts into these many streams of its action and being.

It is with such a definition of life before us that we gladly announce the proposition that Christianity is not a group of doctrines, not a long, hard creed, but is a life. A creed is much like the architect's plan of a house. If competent workmen should follow those plans a house would be the result, so when any one possesses an orthodox creed in his mind as being true, he is in the situation of a man who has plans for a palace or a ship or a home. He has all except the palace or the ship or the home. When any one comes to us boasting over his perfect creed, we should remind him that if he will only live that creed he will become a Christian.

We all remember when the Hungarian patriot journeyed all over our country carrying with him a written constitution of a free state. He even issued bonds in the name of the new republic of Hungary. That parchment was the creed, but inasmuch as a state is not a creed, but a life, the great Hungarian must sit down in sorrow and wait for death to remove him from a world of blighted hope. The creed of the Church is just such a written constitution. It has been read long and loud at all cross-roads, but I will leave it for you all to answer whether we have the house or only the plans of the architect, whether we have the state or only a good constitution for one in some far-off futurity.

It is a most singular fact that in this great temperance reform there is one special multitude of intemperate men, and a large multitude it is too, which sustains full membership in an orthodox Church, in a Church that surpasses all others in asserting the divinity of Christ and the expiatory atonement. No Church can equal it in delineating the pains of hell and the joys of heaven, and yet with all these cardinal doctrines flaunted upon its silk banners and intoned by all its priests, this most profoundly orthodox Church sends forth from its bosom, especially from its Emerald Isle, a swarm of human beings almost wholly ruined by poverty, ignorance, and vice. They land upon our shores by the thousands every week, and against their coming we do not object, for all Christian hearts ought to welcome them from a land of famine and bondage to one of plenty and liberty; but coming, they prove that an orthodox creed no more indicates actual Christianity than poor Kossuth's constitution was equivalent to an enlightened state. The sorrows of Ireland all come from the fact that no Christianity has ever been given them, except that of a complex series of articles; the spirit of life which was in Christ has not been busy these hundreds of years, freeing them from the law of sin and death, but instead of this spirit of Christ's life being preached and acted before them, a hundred articles have been repeated over their darkened minds and enslaved hearts, with the accompaniment, "Believe and go to heaven, or disbelieve and be lost."

In this awful treatment of human souls the Catholic Church did not alone approach Ireland, but accompanied by a vast Protestant Church, which, repeating the same creed, did not exact even that fragment of piety to be found in an intellectual assent, but only so much of the "spirit of life in Christ" as is found in heavy taxes imposed upon the poor to support an idle royalty. Between the Roman Church, which carried nothing to Ireland but words, and the English Church, which sent them nothing but an armed posse to drain rents, the poor island has groaned for hundreds of years under Paul's law of sin and death. But I often think that God at times selects some spot of earth to be an example, and there permits some of man's errors to culminate, that other lands may see the awful outcome of their own religious and social philosophy. What would Ireland not have been to-day, with its rich soil, its perpetual spring, its ocean roads connecting it with all nations, with its great race of Celts and Gauls, which race is the best of all history, if only the Roman and English Churches had gone with a Christianity that was a life, instead of with one which was only forms and taxation? There can be no Christianity without a new spiritual life. Its first move is to rise above intemperance, above all bad passions, above ignorance, above idleness, above barbarism, which is only a general name for sin, and to this end it is a light to enlighten and a spirit to transform; and under these forces the soul becomes freed from the law of sin and death, and rises like Paul up toward the higher being. But instead of going to the Green Isle with this spiritual regeneration, two of the largest Churches in Christendom, the Roman and the English, repaired thither—the former with nothing but a poor belief, the latter with taxes and with the same belief, only modified far enough to become unwelcome. Between both these good Samaritans money and education and virtue and self-respect and industry and hope disappeared; and now all the poor Irish at home and abroad can do is to celebrate each year, in March, the memory of one Christian saint who once touched that island, a thousand years ago. It is to be hoped the story is true, for so few Christians have touched those shores since, that we would better as long as possible cherish this lonely legend.

I have dwelt thus long over Ireland because, as I said, it is only a spot where a philosophy that exalts a creed and depresses a life has come to full maturity, and thus points out the destiny that awaits our land so sure as we fail to make our religion aim at the education and morals of men.

The danger of being misunderstood when one thus speaks about creeds, or of being misinterpreted by those who do not wish to understand, is fully appreciated; but the fact in the case is so true and so alarming that the danger of my being misunderstood is nothing compared with the danger of public morals, if Christ should not be more fully represented as a life. He must lift upward the whole mental nature until all intemperance, all dishonesty, all uncharitableness, shall be loathed as a deep dishonor. Christ must be an education, a refinement, a purity of heart; not a history attested by four evangelists and confirmed by Josephus and Tacitus, and hence believed, but a spirit entering the heart and sweeping away the law of sin and death. An intemperate Christian, or a dishonest Christian, must be confessed to be the real infidel, for whatever his lips may say, his soul is against Christ. There are islands in the Pacific which it is said had no vices until Christians went there; and that awful scourge under which one nation groans, and by which our city is deeply injured, is said to be the peculiar invention and favorite of Christian lands. It will remain so until the whole Church moves from an external history of religion to an internal spiritual state, and makes the spirit of Christ the true test of discipleship, and the sole object of all preaching and of all houses of worship. In this chapter from which our text is taken it is affirmed that "if a man have not the spirit of Christ he is none of His;" but the Church has never believed it, but has offered heaven to misers and drunkards, when once a year they have shown some zeal for an external creed. The difficulty in Christianizing India lies in the pitiable characters revealed there by the British officers and subjects, all of whom have sworn to the thirty-nine articles. The German pietist Tauler was right when he said Christianity is an experience within, and one thought of God is beyond the worth of the external world.

The world has tried external doctrines to the most extreme limit. It has taken the ideas of the Testament, and has stated them in a thousand ways, and has called them everything from Arianism to Calvinism, from Lutherism to Wesleyism, from Romanism to Protestantism, from Mysticism to Quakerism, until the creeds of the Church would form a large volume;

and yet not a soul from the atmosphere of any of these creeds has ever been anything except so far as he cast himself simply upon the spirit of Christ's life, and suffered that vast spirituality to separate him from his body of death, to crush the law, that when he would do good evil was present with him; and whenever any soul has done this he has risen up in the same spiritual beauty, whether he was a Catholic like Fenelon, or a Methodist like Wesley, or a Calvinist like Chalmers—risen the same, because there is no rising at all for a Christian except right up out of the spirit of Christ. Christianity is in man a "well of water springing up," and hence no one can distinguish between the Catholic Massillon and the Protestant Robert Hall, because they came not from an external, changing creed, but from the life of the Lord. Let our sun sink where it may, the same gold gathers about the west in Oregon that hangs out its banners in England or on the mountains of Asia, because the atmosphere is the same and the sun is the same, and the clouds are the same everywhere; and thus true Christians are all one, because they come not from manifold doctrines, but they are the same soul colored by the same Christ, whether he is seen in old Judea or new America.

My friends, we are living in an era of great vices. The fact that there are such vices so sweeping—vices which seek the sanction of law, and which already laugh at the puny arm of religion—should make us doubt whether the ages of simple doctrines do not, by their failure, invite us to a Christianity of life which shall plead for all reforms, and shall by education and a love of the dissolute multitude which shall lead us to espouse whatever will tend to lift them above ignorance and wickedness, help them, not to our long theology, but to such a life of spirituality and purity and moral grandeur as is spread out before them in that golden page of Bethlehem. To build up this "higher life" in the multitude let us omit nothing. From school-house to church, from entreaty to prayer, from reason to divine spirit, from the intercession of man to the intercession of the cross, use all, not in the name of an external history, but in the name of a most radical reform.

"Our course is onward, onward *into light!*
What though the darkness gathereth amain!
Yet to return or tarry, both are vain.
How full of stars when round us dark the night!
Whither return? What flower yet ever might,
In days of gloom and cold and stormy rain,
Enclose itself in its green bud again,
And hide itself from tempest out of sight?"

OLD TESTAMENT INSPIRATION.*

David Swing.

Psalms xxiii and cix.

The Mosaic age presents to the Christian and general student a topic of uncommon interest. The interest is rendered uncommon by the questions of inspiration and policy, and by the entanglement of the Mosaic writings with the questions of geology, and other sciences, on the one hand, and with questions of morals on the other.

Approaching any other old writings, we are permitted to read, and accept or reject, because they are confessedly human; but the contents of the Hebrew books are spread upon a background of inspiration, and this claim excites a clamor and debate.

In our remarks this morning we shall speak of the Mosaic writings only as related to morals, leaving the geological question to future times when that science shall have become more exact. In order properly to estimate the morals of the Hebrew Scriptures, it is necessary to define inspiration, for upon that definition will depend the answer to the inquiry whether the Old Testament is inspired.

If, by inspiration, one is to understand a perfect invasion of the human heart and mind by the Infinite Spirit, so that the human is borne away from itself, and thinks only in the words and thoughts of God, then, we should have no hesitation in saying that there was no such inspiration in the souls of the writers of the Mosaic age. God is perfection. Hence a human mind penetrated by the Deity would deal only in perfect ideas and actions. But, if by inspiration we may understand Divine assistance given to man, such that he became enabled to think wise thoughts and better, and devise useful things above the ordinary thought and utility of the times, then, the Old Testament affords abundant evidence of inspiration.

God never at once thoroughly equips man. Minerva is fabled to have leaped forth full-armed from the brain of Jupiter, but aside from fable there is no record of any such event. The

*A discourse delivered Sunday morning, Nov. 10, 1872, by Prof. David Swing, Pastor of the Fourth Presbyterian Church.

Divine Spirit never creates a perfect man, but sets him going with the permission to become perfect. The plan of God is that of perpetual assistance. He fills the earth with ores, with coals, with the power to produce harvests of grass, fruits and grains, and then endows man with an expansive faculty, such that he can develop the world and himself. The world, as God gave it to His children, is one of opportunities and outfits, and not of completed things.

Inspiration would therefore assume the form of a help rather than of a full occupation of the human intellect and feelings, and would no more be a perfect unfolding of God's whole character than the wild Indian is an expression of God's perfect ideal of the creature man.

Eternity being the time, and immensity the arena of Deity, there would seem demanded a graduated method, such, that to-morrow might always promise something better than yesterday, to-night, or to-day brings. In harmony with such a presumption, nature is full of simple beginnings and grand openings. Coming to inquire about revelation, we should expect the phenomenon of imperfection, but of great help, also, and great progress. A revelation that should wholly relieve man from further effort and inquiry along the path of truth, would be in discord with the economy of earth, for man's success comes from the perpetual struggle into which he is cast by the world's method. The Creator would no more grant man a perfect revelation than He would furnish man with ready made furniture, or houses, or clothing.

In the Mosaic economy, therefore, we must expect the human element to predominate, and to be still engaged in the common struggle after more and better truth. It would be unwise to suppose the Old Testament a perfect image of God — the ideal Infinite. There is no emblazonment of God anywhere. Do you imagine that when you find man in the state of nature — man as seen in the islands of the South Sea, or as seen in the wilds of our America — the red man, you have found an emblazonment of the Deity? By no means. You have found only the place where God has made a beginning; the place, not where God has finished a palace, but where the earth has been broken for a foundation, and where a stake has been driven. Upon earth, when men are about to build a marble structure destined to be full of elegance of finish, and full, perhaps, of works of art, they first build a wide fence about the area, and then descend into the wet earth and work in rough rock. Thus the Creator proceeds in His universe, and there is no perfect manifestation anywhere of His full glory or wisdom.

The Mosaic economy was nothing else than a progress. Earth had come to Polytheism, to Pantheism, to Feticism.

The idea of a Superior Force was universal, but it had not been gathered up into a great central point and perceived to be God. Each thing that had power, such as the sun and moon and sea — each object that was far away, stars and sky — each creature that was terrible, such as serpents and crocodiles — each animal that was very useful, as the cow and the horse, became deities, and were worshipped as such. The air was full of superhuman powers. Disease was a bad spirit. Thus the idea of a superhuman being was broken up into fragments, and was found in a serpent or stone, or in the fire or wind. Under such a discordant belief, morals were discordant, and customs horrible. With a serpent or a crocodile for a deity, man became cruel. He could slay his children, or eat his fellow, for his Fetich was a bloody devourer, and the worship must become such. The slaughter of children became common. Even Rome could crowd her vast amphitheatres in order to see captives eaten by beasts, or slain by each other in contest.

It is necessary for the superhuman power in the air to be called away from the *many* into the *one*. It is necessary to dismiss the sun with its flame, the lightning with its tongue of fire, the serpent with its poison, the crocodile with its sharp teeth. It is necessary to dismiss the iron-hearted Jupiter, and the Apollo with rattling arrows, and Juno full of resentment, and come to a Being, called God, infinite and unchangeable in His being, power, holiness, justice, goodness and truth.

With such a sublime centre, life moves afresh. The serpent becomes only a rude form of brute life. Things thought to be gods sink to the level of the dust, and no longer influence human hearts, passions and hopes and fears, but, instead of these, there is one vast influence, pure and unchanging, drawing all men up to it. The greatest single idea possible to mankind is the idea of God as a Being, only one all-wise, all-good, all-powerful. Looking up to this, nations cast away their barbarism, and the individuals, Elijah-like, ascend in a beautiful chariot.

The Mosaic age was the bearer of this idea. How far it may have known the truth as to geology, I know not, and care not There may be men that know, and men that care, but, amid these indeterminate questions, one thing is clear, that the Hebrew age was the perfect filtration and purification of the idea of God. Perfect as compared with all before it and about it. There is the source of our Christianity and civilization. It was the Hebrew philosophy and its immediate result, Christianity, that swept away the iron Jupiter, and bloody Mars, and revengeful Juno, and all bonds and stakes and stones of the terrible past — swept them away, and gave us the uniform morals and humanity of the nineteenth century.

But, while the Jews were cherishing and developing this idea, they did not cease at once to be men, and become the perfect image of God. From the method of the world thus far, it is probable it will require ten thousand years for humanity to produce a perfect civilization. Six thousand years having already passed, it is perfectly safe to say that four thousand years more will be needed. Such being, in part at least, the fact, the Jews in their brief life could only have moved over part of this vast circle, and must necessarily reveal the ordinary attributes of mankind in the details of their career. Whatever was human custom would be their custom. If wars of extermination were the rule of that age, and were necessary in order to advance the Hebrew Theocracy, then they would appear with Moses and Aaron as leaders, just as naturally, as though Hannibal or Cæsar were leading the Israelites. The age was not one in which the Deity had displaced man, but one in which man was blessed with one or two new truths.

For example, let it be granted that Watt was inspired to invent the steam engine. Mankind needed a new motive power. Unaided, man had failed to reach any thing better than the horse, the ox, or man-power, on land, and than sails on the sea. Watt is at this crisis divinely aided to the discovery of steam. But this would not imply that his engine was perfect, or that anything about it should cease to be human. The machine was rude. A boy stood by to work the valves. Its motion was only in a straight line. It worked a pump, but could not turn a wheel. Here it was in the mines, powerful but imperfect; inspired but incomplete. The inspiration began and ended in a single idea — a simple beginning. The engine was developed until the instrument has reached a beauty and perfection undreamed of by the originator himself. The first instrument is set aside by the new development, and yet, the first one was inspired, and the second one human. Again, the inspiration of Watt's engine not only was imperfect as to the engine, but it did not extend beyond it. The men who worked it were common men. They were profane, they stole, they told falsehoods, they fought, they were more or less indolent, they abused their children and their wives after the fashion of all the colliers and all ignorant classes of that age. And this, too, with the inspired machine in the centre of their daily life.

This illustrates the only intelligible theory of the Mosaic age. It was carrying forward an inspired idea — an idea that was to outlive all Polytheism, and transform the face of society. But the inspiration hung around the idea and did not wander from it. The instant you left the idea, you touched humanity. The people fought and cheated, and held and sold slaves, just as the Greeks and Romans did, and acquired land after the fashion of the barbaric period. But this is no objection to the inspiration of their idea of God. It might as well be objected to the inspiration of Watt's engine that the coal-heavers fought and lived dishonorably. Regardless of the customs of men, the idea of the steam engine was grand on the outset. And so the Mosaic age, regardless of its particulars, was sublime in its crystalization of the ideas of God.

The character of individuals is often a thing distinct from the character of their work. The men that discovered America, or that settled Virginia, may have been freebooters, as some claim, and yet, their vessels may have sailed by a divine inspiration. The inspiration would not include their character, but would look to the future — far off — of America. God is always suffering the individual to fall away, and disappear, leaving behind him something about to become divine.

Thus Moses and all his compeers walked in a human world having one divine element in it. Holding to a true idea of God as a single spirit, eternal and indivisible, they stole land like men at large. Separating Deity from a Fetich, they sold slaves like the old Persians. Appointed to bear religion a few steps onward, they still claimed a plurality of wives like the Philistines, and falsified like the heathen world. But, as on the freebooter's ship, there may have sailed once the civilization of England from the shores of old Rome, or as on the gold-seeking ships of Spain there was borne the coming grandeur of America, an invisible passenger sleeping in the festoons on the vessel's bow, so, in the great Hebrew vessel sailing across the dark flood rolling between the Amalekites and the nineteenth century, there was an invisible passenger of divine spirit and purpose; but the men who worked the sails, and handled the cargo, and cast and heaved the anchor, were tumultuous, sinful seamen, after the fashion of the times.

These thoughts bring me now to the structure of the psalms of David. Many of them being deeply religious, and suitable to all religious hearts everywhere, there are others that belonged only to the days when they were sung. If it was permitted the Israelites to destroy their enemies, and thus establish the better their Monotheism, it was necessary they should sing battle-songs, and that much of their hymnology should be military. In days of an American struggle with England, the song of "The Star-spangled Banner" might be useful and truthful. It might impel men along the best path of the period. In France a few years the "Marseillaise" was rising with power, for it was necessary for the people to check the reckless ambition of Louis Napoleon. These hymns might be confessed to possess a temporary inspiration. That is, their good is unmistakable. But let the world and civilization advance, let war become a crime and a barbarism, let peace become not only an article of religion but a policy of all nations, let all disputes be settled by arbitration and payment of damages, and in that golden age the war songs of America and France become a poor dead letter, and no heart remains so warlike as to sing them.

Thus with such psalms as the one hundred and ninth. They had a temporary significance depending altogether upon the kind of work the Hebrews had to perform. If it was necessary for them to go to battle, it was desirable they should have a battle song, a Marseillaise. If their hands must do bloody work they were entitled to sing a terrific psalm. But the moment the Hebrew method of life passed away, the moment their war for national existence ceased, that moment the one hundred and ninth psalm lost its value. For if the bloody Hebrew war is over, so is its battle-song. There is no logic in perpetuating a war-cry after the war itself has passed away.

But when you read the twenty-third psalm, or a majority of the whole collection, you have not the war-cry of a generation, but the yearnings and feelings of all humanity. Hence I would say that the one hundred and ninth psalm was the good of an hour, the twenty-third psalm is the good of all human life this side the grave.

There is, it seems to me, no other conceivable method of treating the Old Testament than that found in the word *eclecticism.* We must seek out its permanent truths, follow its central ideas, and love them the more because they were eliminated from the barbaric ages with so much sorrow and bloodshed. He that can give the Mosaic age and the old Jewish people only a contemptuous sneer, is a person of little reflection and gratitude. Much as our feelings all rise up against the severity of those ages, yet, in those very times there was being wrought out for us a religion that should introduce Christianity, and thus our morals and our liberty.

Looking back, we perceive not only Washington, and then Luther, and then the old Saxons, and old Romans, and Greeks, but we perceive David and Solomon, and all their grand associates, living and toiling, and dying for you and me—standing with stout hearts and bleeding hands between the low idolatry of primitive man and the civilization of the nineteenth century. David and Solomon were preludes to the blessed Saviour. Faltering in some of their accents, with imperfect music, indeed, they sang a hymn that carried the world sweetly along toward the grand melody that was soon to appear in the Sermon on the Mount, and in the divine chants of the children of Jesus Christ.

SALVATION AND MORALITY.*

DAVID SWING.

Blessed are they which do hunger and thirst after righteousness; for they shall be filled.
Matthew v : 6.

The Sermon upon the Mount may be offered as the text and warrant of the discourse this morning, and from the text you may easily conclude that the subject of remark will be Salvation and Morality.

It is so difficult to make the discriminations demanded by professional theologians, descended often from dark and narrow periods, that we often feel like abandoning forever, not the truths of the Bible, but the hope of saying words that shall please or profit minds that belong to the exact and exacting class in theology. In our own denomination there are so many always ready to complain that "he preaches a religion of morality, he ignores the work of Christ," that one may well hesitate between an utterance that brings complaint and a silence that secures peace. We all love peace. It is the natural wish of most hearts that their life shall be made up of halcyon days, days when no wind ruffles the waters, and when the sun pours upon them in full beauty and warmth. To gratify this wish, there is constant temptation to speak only such words as will blend with the past, and not jar its peaceful sleep. In face of this temptation, we must confess that it does seem high time something were said about a religion of morality, or if the terms be better — salvation and good works.

We must premise by saying that, in our opinion, exactness is impossible in theology. It seems wholly beyond human skill to define faith and charity and salvation with a material exactness. There are instruments by which a measurement of one millionth of an inch may be readily made, but the moment you get away from the material world, this instrument is powerless, and there seems none to take its place. In this poverty of instrumentation, it appears we shall never be able to tell the world just what faith is, just what salvation is, just what

*A discourse delivered in McVicker's Theatre to the Fourth Presbyterian Church, by the Pastor, Rev. David Swing.

the office of the Saviour is, and just what that of man's will and of the Divine Spirit is.

Outside of theology, men have never been able to determine just what literature is, what poetry is, what eloquence is, what the motive of virtue may be, what is the exact value of democracy, or pleasure, or wealth, or education. Paley contends that the greatest happiness is the foundation of morals. Victor Cousin says, "Morals is its own foundation. We do a right thing because it is right."

It would be wonderful if thinking men, by simply passing over into the field of theology, should find a realm full of exactness, and offering the most perfect definitions to any one in the least partial to such pursuits. How is it that the words, literature, eloquence, poetry, civilization, right, are so reluctant to accept of rigid analysis, and that theology is so willing to lie down under the knife of the demonstrators of moral anatomy? How comes it to pass that the question "What is liberty?" or "What is civilization?" will always refuse the world a precise answer, and the question "What is salvation?" may be answered in a moment by the nearest professor in the schools of the church? We recall now the anecdote of science, by which some savan attempted to entrap Franklin, or Columbus, or Pythagoras. "How comes it to pass," inquired Science, "that if a cup be filled to the brim, and then many fishes be put gently into the cup, the water shall not overflow? Instead of explaining the phenomenon, the ideal Franklin or Pythagoras tried the experiment, and the water did overflow.

Thus in our theological world. The question "How comes it to pass that salvation may be so exactly defined?" is to be answered, "It does not come to pass at all. The glass does overflow." The definition, when exact, is so far false; for in order perfectly to define a saved soul, it would be necessary for man to read the judgment of God, and to perceive all that in the last day will be counted in or counted out in the solemn estimate. As it will be the office of God only to assign places to the spirits called away from this life, with Him must rest the detailed facts upon which the sphere of the soul shall be prescribed for the vast hereafter. Hence, the Infinite One only knows the full import of the word salvation, knows its essentials, its limitations; He only knows exactly what hearts will ascend from the scenes of earth up to a supreme bliss.

One of our hymns says with truth,

> There is a time, we know not when,
> A point, we know not where,
> That marks the destiny of men
> For glory or despair.

It is a true thought, but I would not limit the mystery by the idea of time and place only, but also by the quantity and quality of religion in the heart. There is no measurement by which man can determine just the soul that shall receive the smile seen in the words, "Well done, good and faithful servant," just the soul that shall tremble at the sentence, "Depart from me ye accursed."

Thus interpreting the hymn, it becomes to my heart powerful and thrilling —

There is a line, by us unseen,
That crosses every path,
The hidden boundary between
God's patience and His wrath.

Oh, where is this mysterious bourn
By which our path is crossed;
Beyond which, God himself hath sworn
That he who goes is lost?

In this shadow realm we would not wish to throw down the exact response that "he that believes" shall safely pass the mysterious bourn; for faith is such a broad, indefinable word that to substitute it for the term salvation, would be to leave us still in the air obscure. "Faith in Christ," would be a phrase still indefinite, for not only has faith many forms, but many forms also attach to the person of Christ. He was a sacrifice, but sacrifice has many significations. He was an example. He was a mediator. He was an unfolding of the divine image. Faith in Christ is a phrase which is at once seen to be made of words that are like the bits of colored glass in the kaleidoscope, forming many pictures and all very beautiful.

The faith of a little child in Christ, would differ essentially from the faith in Jesus of a person come to education and deeper thought. In the child's estimate there could enter no analysis of the Saviour in the theological sense of the term. His offices of atoning lamb, of example, of image of God, would all be crowded out of the young heart by the enthusiastic reception of Christ as a loving, glorified, heavenly friend. If to such a child what is called salvation could come, then must we confess that salvation must elude scholastic definition, and make of itself new pictures according to the hand that turns the magical glass. The words must possess an elasticity greater than will be admitted by the schools founded to promulge an exact idea.

Now, this refusal of salvation to be defined in language rigidly exact and sharp, ought to make us all very unwilling to separate it in any way from good works. There is such a growing together of these two ideas in the whole New Testament that any separation of them seems an act of ignorance or vandalism toward the life and history of Christ. The entire Sermon upon the Mount is a union of morals and salvation.

It is the most careful unfolding of a religion of morality that was ever uttered or read upon earth. From its outburst, in which heaven is assigned to the poor in spirit and pure in heart, to its last verse, where doing good works is the foundation of rock, upon which every man's hope should be built, the divine discourse marches along to the key-note of morality.

There is no evading the significance of the fact that in all the days and hours of Christ's life upon the earth, the doctrine of good works was the cardinal idea in every speech, and even in the most solemn prayer of Gethsemane. Into the brief, model prayer, into which we may suppose this divine intelligence gathered up the most useful petitions, he taught mankind, that to forgive and be forgiven, to be delivered from temptation and evil, were the blessings needed by the soul, and hence, the essence of its salvation.

Between us and a salvation, the teachings of Christ about an upright life, stand with such a broad depth and sublime height, that it would seem like presumption and egotism in man to announce for the soul a safety in which good works should perform no prominent part. If what is called in exact theology, "faith," is the sum and substance of salvation, it is almost wonderful that the great Captain of our salvation, instead of setting forth this idea in His earthly discourses, in almost every case gave the impulse and sanction of His career to the doctrine of an upright, religious life. With the words of Jesus before us, far be it from us ever to utter a word that would seem to give hope of heaven to a soul not building up a personal righteousness.

The alarm expressed by many pulpits, that many are relying too much upon a life of morality, seems to jar at once with all the words of the Saviour, and with the events of the sad times in which our country lives.

In this Credit Mobilier phenomenon, I see no tendency on the part of public men to base their soul's salvation on good works. That list of names that is at the same time associated with the church and with the acceptance of bribes, does not seem in the least injured by any reliance upon good works for salvation. Their hope of heaven must be based upon faith alone. The righteousness they dream of must be wholly an imputed righteousness. In presence of Sin, bursting forth in high and low places, like as plague issuing from the plains of India; Sin, with one hand full of bribes, the other dripping in blood, we should tremble, as a servant of Christ, to utter one word that would warn mankind against placing too high an estimate upon the value of a sinless life. Upon all the horizon we cannot behold any encroachment of this evil. The only persons visibly wedded to the moral life, are certain followers of William Penn, and in the group of bribe-holders, between Kansas and the Atlantic, no one of these "mere moralists" seems visible. Caution against salvation by good works would, therefore, seem premature. With the Catholics buying righteousness with a price, so many pardons for a sinful soul, and with many Protestants, warned against placing confidence in anything but faith, the time for being alarmed at any over-development of Quaker morality, appears not yet to have come.

Standing amid the scenes that surround us all to-day, if there be any connection spoken of in the Bible as existing between a man's morals and his destiny, this would seem like the year and our country the place, in which all such relationships should be brought out in all the theological schools and rostrums in the land. There has never been a time when the morality of the Quakers could be so well endured. Would that there might be, in all the schools of the land, a Quaker professorship of honesty endowed along with the chair of saving faith. Unable as we all may be to see what influence upon heaven a salvation by help of good works might exert, whether it would leave that blessed realm to be a solitude, it must be confessed that actual human righteousness would be very valuable to this star and this generation.

If Christ by His death wrought out a salvation for man, man's heart must be the prize bought with the sacred life and death. There is no salvation for a sinful soul except a pure life. Hence, if Christ effectually assists man to this pure soul, He is man's Saviour, and the pure soul is the salvation. If good works are the salvation, Christ is still the Saviour. Hence, salvation by good works and salvation by Jesus the Redeemer are so inseparably blended that any effort to separate, must result in an insult to the Cross on the one hand, and to the Sermon on the Mount on the other. It cannot be that Christ would save a race in their sins, but from their sins, and hence, the flight from sin is always a flight to the bosom of God. This is therefore the essence and soul of Christianity, this upward flight.

If to us, lost in a wilderness, without a sun, nor a star, nor a path to guide, there comes a benevolent hermit, a dear Mentor, and leads us to the right path, and sets out faces homeward, he is at once our saviour; but no perfect salvation will come from our going that path. Our "going" and the Mentor combine in the escape, and yet he lives in memory as the kind saviour of our bewildered hearts.

Thus Christ may be the Saviour of mankind, and yet leave our morality as the final embodiment of His salvation. All the work of Christ contained in the word Calvary, or atonement, is only the objective part of the soul's rescue, whereas, man's own personal righteousness is the subjective salvation, the thing for which the other exists. Good works are the explanation of Calvary.

The words and life of Christ show that what He most desired, was the spiritual perfection of His children. "Be ye perfect, even as your Father in heaven is perfect," was the ruling wish of His heart. All His eloquence was aimed at, not simply acts of sin, but even sinful thought. In the transcendent light of His morals, the Ten Commandments faded like a snow-drop upon the bosom of ocean. The heaven of Jesus was both a purity and a place, and hence, the final analysis of salvation will show us a sinless soul, at one with Christ, as He and the Father are one.

There is no conflict, perhaps, between Paul and the Saviour. I use the word "perhaps" only as a further confession of the impossibility of determining with scientific exactness the whole of Paul's thought on the one hand, and the whole of the Saviour's thought on the other. Assuming inspiration, there of course is no conflict. But not thus begging the question and appealing only to rationalism, there seems no discord in the two strains of music. Paul unfolds salvation from without. He tells what is necessary outside of man. Hence Calvary and law and imputation and satisfaction come upon his horizon at all hours. There the Jewish altar is transformed into a cross. The first Adam and second Adam meet. The past sins of humanity are gathered up mountain high, and a price is to be paid for them, paid in blood and death. While these scenes of objective salvation are pictured in intense colors upon the sky of the saint, the scenes of the subjective salvation are passing along through the mind of the Saviour — souls full of virtue, full of brotherly love, souls from which even evil thoughts have been banished forever. Paul is busy with the paths to a destiny; Christ with the beautiful destiny itself. There is no necessary conflict, but Christ remains as always everywhere the greater. He never halts in any vestibule, or sits down upon a confine. He passes into the holy places of the soul and utters the final wisdom and prayer and destiny of the poor mortals waiting for His words.

In this salvation which hath two parts, the way and the going in that way, the hand is rash indeed that would separate the human character from the salvation. In order to do this it is not only necessary to abandon all the Gospels of Christ, but it is necessary also to misunderstand Paul and torture him upon the rack of a system. In a world where the absence of integrity, the absence of righteousness is so remarkable as to fill society with alarm by day and by night, and in an era, too, where what is called salvation by faith alone has been crowded forward with wonderful ability and success, as to acceptance, it seems high time the scholastic meaning of salvation were made to expand until it should receive into its polluted heart the Sermon on the Mount and the morals of Jesus. The faith demanded by this sinful race is one that will not simply look upon a price for its sins, but upon a career of individual virtue, a faith that believes in Christ, not only upon Calvary, but in the Gospels, Christ not only in Mosaic types, but Christ in the spotless purity recorded by Matthew and St. John. A religion is needed that will not dare tell mankind that works are of no significance, that will not dare cast contempt upon any righteousness except an imputed one, a religion that will not dare spurn the entire life and words of Him who spake as never man spake. This is not a salvation without Christ. The difficulty will be found to be that it has too much of Christ in it. To the teachings of Calvin and Luther it adds the teachings of the Saviour as an important supplement.

The divine Jesus with His morality, with His curse upon one who even called his brother Raca, with his prayer "Be ye perfect," with His benediction for him who did the least commandment and taught men so, with His whole career full of man's subjective salvation, is an object too vast to be swept from the Christian sky by the besom of any school, past or to come. Be you anywhere, my friend, in the journey of life; in youth, or middle life, or old age, do not suffer any voice to confuse your heart as to the need of a personal obedience rendered the teachings of the Saviour. The precise meaning of salvation may elude your power of definition. You may not be able to find that line that crosses every path—

> "The hidden boundary between
> God's patience and His wrath,"

but whatever darkness may gather around you, amid the obscure definitions of men, there will always be in the imitation of Jesus Christ a place where no shadow can come. A religion that will make the Sermon on the Mount play a second part in your earthly career, comes it under any name, Calvinist, Methodist, Baptist or Catholic, that religion decline, or abandon so far, and draw nearer to Him who knew better than all the schools, wherein lies the best destiny of the soul.

All through the life of Christ the music of heaven sounded to the pure in heart, and an awful thunder rolled in all the sky, over the spirit that sinned in deed and in thought; and when a generation after the Saviour's death, the heavens opened to the vision of St John, and this divine Being stood a radiant star on the border of earth, there came the same music again for the virtuous, the same thunder in the futurity of the wicked. "Blessed are they that do His commandments, that they may have right to the tree of life, and may enter in through the gates of the city; for without are dogs and sorcerers and murderers and idolaters and whosoever loveth and maketh a lie." Here the morals of Jesus return to us in awful significance. Let us not add to nor take away from the words of the prophecy of this book.

We have come to evil days—days when public men who stand forth as members of the Christian church, even of the churches called orthodox, hesitate not to carry in the same heart a salvation by faith and a willingness to receive bribes. Among the public men now charged with glaring dishonor there may be some who can establish innocence, but the awful fact is everywhere confessed, that there are thousands of Christians who are getting their salvation by faith and their fortunes by rascality. If the parties could be found who have in the past brought about this divorcement between salvation and good works, they should be urged to come forward and confess their sin before the nineteenth century, so injured in all the sacred places of its soul. In the name of injured virtue, in the name of public calamity, come and coming, they should read and preach, not only the grand philosophy of Paul, but the still grander morals of Jesus Christ.

There is a Christianity that will save the world. It has not only a faith, but it has a morality as essential as its faith. It not only says "Believe and be saved," but it assigns damnation to him who leads a wicked life. There is a Christianity that will not only fill heaven with saints, but earth with good citizens. In it Paul and Christ are not rudely separated, and the human placed above the divine, but the morals of the Gospels come back to mankind, and the anxiety for faith is no greater than the hungering after righteousness.

In the pictures and images of the Cross seen in all homes in this era of tenderer sentiment, there is often to be seen a garland of flowers, surrounding the cruel wood in their loving embrace. Emblems of life and death indeed! but may they be to us always, emblems of the Sermon upon the Mount, inwreathing the atonement, forming a part of the indefinable salvation—inseparable. The Christ that gave the world the Cross, wove also the garland of morality that completes its adaptation to the wants of man.

THE WOMAN'S TEMPERANCE REVIVAL.*

DAVID SWING.

"She hath done what she could."—*Mark xiv: 8.*

Much as the present boasts of its liberality as to woman, a liberality expressed in both statute law and public sentiment, yet when one turns to a study of the facts, he closes up history uncertain whether woman is as free in America as she was in Greece, or even in Palestine. It is probable that a more universal education leads a larger number of female minds to the front, to stand among the writers and thinkers and moral workers, but that the woman of our age possesses any great legal or social advantage over the woman of the best ancient nations, is a question not so easily determined. The presumption in all young and in all sanguine souls is in favor of the present, for with such the past seems only a good thing to have moved away from, a good region for man's infancy but inadequate for adult mental action. Against this presumption, however, facts rise up, so far as woman's history is concerned, and both in sacred Palestine and in Rome and Athens there are to be seen pictures of life which may well make us doubt whether the boasts of our times along this special path are founded upon fact or only upon self-complacency. Although in Palestine woman had never reached the intellectual power and genius which she had attained in Greece, and perhaps not the social distinction, yet in that land where the patriarchial system had made the father and the son so prominent, there are historic scenes in which the Marys and the Marthas and other grand names are very prominent in the public and private works of religion. It would seem from Paul's restriction upon woman's work, that there must have been places or congregations where this second ereature in the scale of creation was presuming to be first, and thus the letters of Paul become a mirror in which we perceive the great liberty of Mary and Martha in that day, mirrored not as desirable but as a fact. The publication of a law against a certain course of conduct is proof that such conduct was on the horizon threatening to become universal. Thus the restricting law of Paul confesses the surrounding liberty of woman; and aside from that law there is evidence that she must have possessed and exercised great power in the early Church. The whole history of primitive Christianity is full of

* Sermon delivered in Fourth Presbyterian Church, February 22, 1874.

names and sketches of active women, if not preaching women, at least of women whose words and deeds were a confessed agency in the first onward movement of the new faith. Christ was attended everywhere by the faithful matrons, and upon the pages of subsequent history the name of the great Augustine is scarcely more conspicuous than the name of Monica, his mother. So the names of Chrysostom, St. Basil, St. Gregory, and Theodoret are associated with the names of their mothers who equaled these illustrious sons in education and active piety. Helena, Flacilla, St. Pulcheria, and Placidia, are names which have come down to us covered with the glory of an association with the teaching and defense of the faith. There was an order of ministering women in the apostolic Church whose duties seem to have been to teach and visit, and to fill indeed about such an office as is now filled by our city missionaries and evangelists. Aside from this study of fact, there are two considerations which might make us infer "a priori" the wonderful liberty and activity of woman in the early Church. The first consideration is that the Roman empire had in the lifetime of Christ, or very near that date, wholly emancipated her as to state law, and had made her the equal of her husband in all particulars. She could make contracts. Her father's property came to her alone, and hence the satirical poets of that period often in comedy brought upon the stage the character of some husband who was borrowing money of his wife and paying her large interest. In those days the Roman empire was the world. Its laws were the laws of all the lands that were washed by the Mediterranean, and its customs were the standard customs; and hence the Christian Church rising up in that atmosphere would naturally give to its female membership the great, surrounding Roman liberty.

A second consideration is to be found in the internal character of Christianity. If ever there was a religion, actual or only dreamed of, which seemed by its doctrines and methods to invite woman to be its advocate, the religion of Christ is that one among all the world has seen. Christ, in His character and in His teachings and in His work, seems to tell mankind that the religion of violence and terror had passed by. From Sinai mankind had moved over to Mt. Sion; and, away from the thunderings and lightnings, had pitched their tents among trees full of flowers and fruit, and under heaven's sweeter sunlight. While the Hebrew religion was often called upon to move against the infidel nations with fire and sword, its servants were necessarily men of war, with iron chariots and many a spear; but when Christ came and arrested all violence, and transformed an army of warriors into a prayer-meeting, and converted the sword of steel into a "sword of the spirit," and throwing down the heavy shield of mêtal gave the soldier "the shield of faith," and plucking from the forehead the helmet of brass, placed there the "helmet of salvation," then, in that sublime spiritualizing of religion, woman seems to have been divinely called from shadow into light. The religion of masculine attributes alone had been revoked, and one had been given for all humanity, and especially given to the care of any division of the human family which might lie nearest to its own tenderness and world-wide sympathy. When religion threw away all violence, when it announced faith, hope, and charity as its great spiritual states to which the world must come, when it reared the cross as its symbol, and hailed such a being as Christ as its only guide and impulse, it especially called to its aid forever that being who is by nature nearer to a reform which advances by kindness, and who, by all her thoughts and sentiments and sacred interests, stands nearer to this divine, central figure of the Testament. Thus the universal liberty and equality which the Roman empire had established, and the fragrance of which must have been wafted all along those sea-washed states, indicate to us that the woman of the early Church must have acted in the name of those broad rights; and then when to this legal and social status we add the internal character of Christianity, all doubt passes, and we easily behold in the primitive Church a position and an activity of woman which perhaps shames the laws and customs of our country, and the humble place she fills in our efforts to reform the multitudes at home and abroad. When, therefore, we all thus look back and recall these facts, and to these considerations add the long list of names, not only of those who toiled for Christ, between the Mary of the first century and the St. Helena of the fourth, but that vast throng of sisters who died the martyr's death, and whose names are graven to-day only upon the Infinite heart, we may well wonder, and not without some misgiving, whether in respect to God's sanctuary, woman enjoys in our nineteenth century the social liberty and the encouragement to usefulness which she enjoyed when Constantine was emperor of Rome. Although society at large has made immense progress since that day, yet there may be here and there a path along which the feet of this progress have not run; and as often families flying from fire or flood forget some most precious thing, taking with them the less valuable, so often nations, full of progress in fact and spirit, often forget some branch of reform, and leave the slave, or the enchained woman, or the child, or some useful art unthought of for a thousand years. It is possible that the feudal system and the monastic system, and then the puritan system, which culminated in the blue laws, drove women back into retirement, from which, at the bidding of wealth and luxury, she comes forth at last a creature of fashion, rather than a full member of thinking and acting society. Be the facts and causes what they may, it does appear that woman's relations to Christianity are little better in the nineteenth than they were in the second or fourth centuries. The words of the text, "She hath done what she could," can only be applied to an individual here and there; but as to the vast female army, the bad customs of society, the irony of men, the overgrowth of dress as a pursuit, and the temptation which riches offer to idleness,—all these stand between woman and the fulfillment of the Scripture which praised the poor devotee who gave her precious gift to the Lord. No age thus far has permitted woman to do what she could.

In the days now passing we all witness a new spectacle, that of an attempted temperance reform conducted in a strange manner and wholly by woman. This movement has assumed such a magnitude, and is so sincere and earnest and religious, that it merits from all who are only the spectators a calm and careful investigation before they approve or condemn. And it is in the spirit of a sincere inquiry I am submitting all these thoughts to-day. The preliminary remarks as to the position of woman in the days nearest to Christ have a bearing upon the question of the hour, for if Christianity set forth as an entreaty, as a pleading with the wicked; set forth not from the porch of philosophy so much as from the recesses of a divine and human heart; if its solicitude for the sinful was to be even unto tears, then when woman is pleading with the man who sells drinks, full of poison for soul and mind and body, however far she may be standing from our approval or from American ideas of propriety, she certainly is not standing very far from the gospel and presence of Jesus Christ. It is more than questionable whether we may set up the peace of our homes and the etiquette of our parlors, or the indifference of our counting-rooms as a standard by which we are to award to this uprising an estimate of merit. It is doubtful whether the pulpit itself has not become so wedded to old theology and so separated from human welfare of earth, dreaming only of that in heaven, that its first impulse may often be false, asking for peace to come to this sea of new, strange storm. In order to judge rightly this movement, it is no doubt necessary that we all pass up into the higher atmosphere of the world's Savior, and look down upon these pleading ones from that height which is sacred with not only the tears but with the poured out blood of Him who plead for a world. There has never come a reform in a manner acceptable to established customs of the drawing-room: for the genius of the latter is peace, while the atmosphere of the former is at least that of great unrest. Neither Luther, nor Peter the Great, nor the great Mme. Guyon, nor the shouting Methodists, nor the itinerent Whitfields has dared consult the etiquette of the marble palaces or marble homes, but have been compelled to overlook the wishes of fashion and placid culture, and draw warrant and inspiration from the overwhelming calamities of mankind. There is much in the new temperance uprising which jars like a discord against my own feelings, and you all will make, perhaps, a similar confession; but I make my confession remembering that just thus have all peace-loving souls been jarred in all ages, and from Paul to Luther, all these reformers have been looked upon by the adjacent citizen-soul as being "mad by much learning," or possessed of a devil, whereas they spoke the words of truth and soberness. This discord which rises in our feelings to-day disappears in our philosophy. Rising above our personal prejudices, we see an evil, the greatest now known to earth, attacked by those who have suffered the most from its ravages, and who can look to the future as to only a continuance of their long sorrow. This is the briefest statement of the case. Let us make a wider, fuller statement of the grave affair. It does not come within the grasp of any mind to express in words the length and breadth of this world-wide curse, but it is permitted us to see some vague outline of this awful scourge. In our own land it consumes a thousand millions of dollars a year; turns that much of wealth or labor away from education, and morals, and home-comfort, and from all the arts, and from all the Christian and human virtues, and visits the effects of this immense diversion of money upon the innocent of each generation. But if the use of these liquors were only a vast withdrawal of labor from useful paths, the world could endure the loss. If this thousand millions of labor were simply destroyed, men could forgive and forget; but on the opposite, it is absolutely applied to the increase of public ignorance, public vice, public crime, and public unhappiness.

Our city congratulates itself that henceforth it will have $50,000 a year for the purchase of books, and is delighted to dream of the citizens who will borrow good books from this great free library; but while this sum is being disbursed the citizens who seek the poisonous cup will spend $14,000,000 in this city alone; and the army which will march up to the bar will every day in the year be more than 50,000 strong. But this city is only a measuring unit of the nation, and is repeated in the whole country one hundred times. Philadelphia spends $30,000,000, New York $60,000,000 a year, and from all the saloons in the land, in city and village, go 5,000,000 drinkers each day, and from that multitude five hundred and fifty persons fall each day into the drunkard's grave. We would that these figures were permitted of God to be the banks of this river of wretchedness over which the wave could not flow, but oh no! the laws of society compel us to see a deeper wrong, for as from a pestilential march a plague rushes out and strikes the whole family, the whole city, and makes new Memphis or old London all weep, so this mania of drink passes from the manhood which enters the charnel houses over to the mother, the wife, the children at home, and tearing down the rose-vine from the window, and removing the food from the table, and the clothes from the wife and children, and putting out the fire upon the hearth, it spreads over all these faces the paleness of coming death, thus hinting that home with its former joys is being transformed into a tomb, of hope at first, and soon of life itself.

Having glanced now at the great calamity against which woman has at last risen in a deep earnestness, let us recall also the fact that it has been into her soul this evil has been pouring most of its grief for a hundred years. Her home, her brother, her father, her husband, her children, her whole world has been ravaged by this one vice more than all others combined into one. And out into this same atmosphere we expect her still to send her sons and to see to it that they shall come home at night without injury for twenty-one years, and shall reach full manhood without having agonized her heart or threatened society by crime against its laws, or by sin against God. In circumstances which, because so familiar, have ceased to be appalling, it need not be wondered at that woman, weary of law which men have not the moral power to pass, nor, if passed, to execute, has begun once more the general crusade against an evil which will not of itself ever abandon her home, her brother, her children.

It may be that her efforts will exhaust itself in one springtime as to its present form, but inasmuch as in the past third of a century this temperance reform has been wide-spread and active, we can only look upon the scene of the present as one more protest from reason and Christianity, in a long series of protests which will no doubt come, in louder and deeper accents, while this vice remains on earth. This is a foe we shall not dare neglect. It will more and more force itself upon the attention of legislature, and press, and courts, and pulpit. It is the "irrepressible conflict," the "impending crisis" of the passing age, and if the hymns and the prayers of tens of thousands of women shall only make the merchant look up from his ledger, and the fashionable lady look away from her jewels, and the pulpit look away from its abstraction, and the "vain repetitions," and all citizens turn and see afresh and in awful truthfulness the curse of the land, so dear in its liberty, not a hymn will have been sung in vain in all these days and nights. No evil has yet fallen except by long-repeated blows, well struck by the children of men. Earth has always been a battle-field in which mind and soul have reached their development and crown by a warfare against foes which seem to have come into life under the very cradle in which our infant world was first rocked. Under the long struggle against kingcraft, a battle that reached from Leonidas to Lincoln, liberty has gradually unfolded itself, as though a strange flower, asking two thousand years for elaborating its color and perfume from the deep blue air. Thus, also, our improved religion has come from amid long insults and varied follies, and even through seas of blood, up to a condition in which God begins to be unveiled as a Father in heaven. But one of the first acts of this religion was to rear a cross. Thus all reforms advance by successive steps of labor and sorrow. That peace which settles over all your homes is not a token to you that all is well in the wide world without, but is perhaps only the sweet refuge into which the mind and heart can fly for rest, but from which they come forth again to resume the life-long struggle with some defiant host. Crucifixion is the word that indicates the world's genius, while peace points out its final destiny. It is, therefore, more than possible, that before the moral forces of society shall make such progress against intemperance, the composure of the boudoir and the whole theory of woman as an ornament alone, or as a domestic, will need to be crucified, and her mental and moral force set free from that bondage of fashion and repose which has been to her a "body of death." In looking upon this new adventure, let us remember that when woman has desired to enter the pulpit we have told her not to come there, and have reminded her of the immense moral field apart from its special office; and when she has knocked at the doors of all the professions, we have again reminded her of the breadth of the world aside from all such paths of employment; and when she has wished to influence all public morals by seeking the right to vote, we have again hastened to assure her that the realm of usefulness is wide, apart from any human relation to the ballot-box; and now, when at last she ventures forth, without pulpit, without profession, without suffrage, but clothed with that moral influence about which the public men have discoursed so long and so sweetly too, perhaps the time for silence on our part, if not for loud approval, has come, because a complaint here might indicate that all past restriction of woman had been only a prejudice instead of a philosophy.

The results of this uprising will be these: Multitudes of the young will this year keep back from the intoxicating cup; hundreds of villages, where all know each other by name, will form a temperance friendship which will purify their home atmosphere for years to come; our towns and villages having been morally improved, the ruin in the cities will still leave the nation a moral hope in the nobler millions outside; the hope of America being not in its cities but in its almost infinite country life, come and yet to come. Rising up out of religion, by its impulse and following its entreaty, this commotion will go far to compel sects to stand upon one level, and will compel the pulpit to abandon the endless definition of Christianity in favor of an application of its blessedness to the strong men bowing beneath a dreadful vice, and to the hearts of their families bowing under hunger and cold and all private neglect and public disgrace. After so long a time the use of Christianity will now follow its discovery. From woman the cause will pass to the columns of the newspaper, and to the legislative halls, and to the bench of the judge, and bosoms of the jury. Hence we cannot but hope that this awakening will go forward, spreading out like a storm cloud over parched fields in June, and that whereas in the dark ages crusades were made in the name of Christianity in search of only a tomb in dead rocks, where at best nothing ever had been but dust, and as now a few devotees are making pilgrimages to the crypt of some phantom saint, may it be the glory of the women of the nineteenth century that they are making their pilgrimages to rescue, not an empty tomb from infidels, but souls from death, and are chanting their hymns, not where some old name is carved on a rock, but to living hearts made in the image of God, and capable of nobleness here and blessedness in the life to come.

DEATHS OF CHIEF JUSTICE CHASE AND JOHN STUART MILL.*

David Swing.

"One star differeth from another star in glory."—*1 Corinthians xv : 41.*

This passage comes often into mind when we observe the diversity of character reached by eminent men living and dying in our sight. The excellence possible to human life never reveals its whole self in any one soul, but seems to divide itself up into fragments and to parcel out these fragments to the care of different hearts. As a kind father surrounded by dutiful children, coming at last to the end of life, makes a final will and testament, dividing up his immense estate to the dear children, so that each has a part, thus nature, rich in all the shapes of genius, talent, and virtue, portions out her immense fortune, and many children beloved come away from her presence carrying some precious gift.

The soil that grows men is much like the soil that grows plants and flowers. This literal soil, lying in its blackness beneath the sun, is ready to produce an oak or rose, a clambering vine or a violet. Often we find in June by some stream a rich spot, which with rare prodigality has sent upward a whole bouquet of species, and colors, and perfumes. The soil that grows men is such. They emerge from it with different shadings of intellect and sentiment, and taste and genius.

The illustration of Paul, that one star differeth from another in glory, finds an increased meaning in the modern time, for astronomy has discovered that some of them are suns that shine with a pink, or emerald, or amber light. And hence the planets around these suns are not bathed in a white light like our day, but in a flood of pink, or gold, or amber.

The human soul presents this variation of glory, and hence fills the spectator with an outlook that never wearies with any monotony. Thousands of minds come and go surrounded with and sending forth their own peculiar light.

If you would realize this truth you need only look upon those who have just gone from earth, for there is always something in the word death that causes the peculiar tint or color of a

*Sermon delivered at McVicker's Theatre, May 18, 1873.

soul to flash up suddenly before us. The solemnity and sorrow of the tomb arrest both our attention and our sympathy, and for the first time we see the image of the soul that has gone hence. The grave, though full of literal darkness, is full of spirit light. The soul becomes most visible to us when it has entered that great shadow. The recent months have afforded us frequent opportunities for this full view of great souls in their rich variety. The hunger for empire flashed forth in the spirit of Louis Napoleon. A worship of the common people and a wonderful industry and information was visible in the memory of the great editor who died last autumn in the sorrow of defeat. A noble form of Christianity, perhaps one of the best embodiments it has enjoyed in our generation, may be observed now in the pale image of Bishop McIlvaine. Uprightness and moderation, and devotion to free principle are evident in the character of Chief Justice Chase, while all that was most intellectual, and dignified, and powerful in the human mind, shines forth now from the name of John Stuart Mill. How these stars differ from each other in glory!

It has long been the custom of our land in its religious press, and in its pulpit also, to draw whatever lessons they could from the great soldiers or politicians that pass away in their presence. This partiality comes in part from the public benefits that descend direct from such men, and from the absence of such characters as the world now laments in the name of Stuart Mill. There is no evident reason why we should all speak of a great soldier, or great editor, or great Chief Justice, and pass in silence a man great in his acquisitions in his rational faculty, in his humanity, in his morals, in his disposition, and in his domestic life. It would not be fitting this sacred day should I speak of this illustrious man in his relations to logical forms and political systems, and metaphysical inquiries, for mankind has set apart six days of seven for reflection and all toil in these departments of thought; but it will seem becoming the hour if I shall recall to your minds some of those points in the life and character of Mr. Mill, at which he came into contact with the world of religion. Into the world of Christianity proper he never entered, but in the splendor of an intellect which revealed a divine origin in his devotion to his brother man, in his elevation above the world's vices and strifes, in his love of truth, and in his domestic life, he illustrated powerfully the ideal humanity pictured in the pages of the New Testament.

The Scriptures are full of delineations of character. From the writings of Solomon to the sermon upon the mount, and to Paul's letter to the Romans, there is a perpetual effort to paint a human character in such lines that society may not mistake the good God has set before it, and in reaching which it will find its perfect success and happiness.

After Solomon had exhausted his maxims, Christ came, saying, Blessed are the pure in heart, the merciful, the peacemakers. And then Paul comes with many a chapter of summing up of human virtues attainable in this life. The reader of the Bible will see that character is the object of all these earthly years, the thing to be sought by all alike from king to subject, from philosopher to child. Such being the life-work of man, he may well gaze upon any beauty and impressiveness of character, come whence it may, in politics or philosophy, or in the humblest walks of earth. Even if Stuart Mill stood nominally outside of the Christian religion, yet there is a sense in which he stood, not by choice, but by necessity, within the boundaries of the New Testament. It is within the power of an individual to reject the special doctrines of a religion; but if that religion has moulded his country for centuries in all its morals and aspirations, then each individual born into that atmosphere is colored with its hues, however much he may repudiate its cardinal dogmas in after life. It is possible for a free will to expatriate one's self from one's country, but go where he may, he will always be the Englishman or American of his formative years. Lady Hester Stanhope tried to escape her country, weary as she was of its political griefs, but in the mountains of Lebanon, in Arab dress, and with only Arabs around her, she was still only an Englishwoman. In Christian lands Christianity, besides being a set of dogmas, is also an atmosphere, and hence those who at last feel called upon to deny the propositions most difficult of belief continue still the children of the place, and if they do not carry the public baptism upon their foreheads, they bear the Christian character in their heart. Hence, to find a beautiful character outside the Christian Church may yet be to find a good illustration of Christian ideal and Christian destiny, for the ideal becomes a public inheritance, and flows beyond the walls of the church, as the light of the cottager's lamp pours out of the window, far away from the loved family group. Of this eminent man a prominent passion was his love of truth. To know the facts in the common affairs of life was so deep a wish in his soul that it became a passion so strong that all other passions died around it as the shrubs of the forest die when the oak begins to overshadow them. In his writings we perceive a heart without enmity, without partizanship, moving along in the vast sea of truth, occupied wholly in search of a shore habitable by the pilgrim humanity. One of our own leading statesmen, having been asked why he never became angry, replied that he could not afford it. Life was too short to be consumed in part by such a passion.

Mr. Mill's style is the picture of a sincere intellect from which all malice had been eliminated, all language of abuse, and into which had been gathered the breadth of a Plato, the learning of a Milton, and the humanity of a Wilberforce. In the careers of such gifted men as Theodore Parker and Charles Sumner, there is so much partisanship and individual pride that the pursuit of truth with them seems too much like a contest for office or fame. The heart that reads these writings has at last such feelings as must have filled the bosoms of the Romans seated at their gladiatorial shows, but reading Stuart Mill you feel that the light around you is not that of lightning, but of a morning sun shining not as any terror, but in benevolence.

If, therefore, the Bible speaks of truthfulness; if Solomon declared the glory of just balances; if the gospels speak of our being without guile; if another sacred writer said, "He that would see good days let him refrain his tongue from evil and his lips that they speak no guile," we may call to memory this English name and know what all this Scripture signified.

It was this love of truth that made Mr. Mill such a lover of liberty. Not only must the unbiased seeker of truth naturally become a lover of personal liberty, on the ground that such freedom makes the pursuit of all truth of government and science and religion possible, but he must love it because all despotism is itself a falsehood—a fraud—a crime.

The world of truth being too large for any one foot to travel over, it is parceled and assigned in districts to different men. While Tyndall seeks the truth of the inanimate world, and while science at large seeks the truth of nature, it was the province of Mr. Mill to seek the truth of human conduct as pertaining to the individual or society. Hence, loving truth, he further dignified his name by developing the truth of conduct rather than of geology or mechanics, or of material things. This noble path led him to cast himself into the study and development of civil and spiritual liberty. All the falseness and cruelty of tyranny in State and Church stands forth in all its deformity. The light of Mr. Mill's reason is so powerful that it dispels all the fogs of centuries and fully reveals the world of freedom long dreamed of but unseen. The few tears we were all accustomed to shed over Galileo and a few martyrs he multiplies into a great rain and sheds them over the human race up to the last hour of yesterday. Our tears fell only for a black man in chains; his fell wherever a subject was slave of a king, or wherever woman was the slave of her employer or her husband. His judgment was simply universal, and as just as is possible in any one man in this generation. England had in his sight imprisoned a man of perfect integrity, for uttering his disbelief in some Christian tenets, and had forbidden a foreigner from testifying against a thief because he confessed that he held no particular religious persuasion. Mr. Mill found a thousand Galileos where the Church had supposed there was but one, and his calm eloquence and logic, poured out for a generation, fought and won over again the battle of personal freedom—not for an astronomer, but for a race. Unquestionably, freedom is the only soil upon which educated men can grow. Bondage is at once the enemy of intellect and religion. Men cannot grow where they are cramped either by a thing or by a fixed system. If, therefore, the day shall come, and come it no doubt will, when the advent of reason shall have overthrown the falsehood in Romanism and Protestantism, and when the enthronement of individual liberty shall have made the English establishment shakes hands with the Dissenter, and the Jew sit down in friendship with the Christian. Much of this humane brotherhood will go back for its origin to that name written this month upon the grave. It has often been necessary, in the history of the Christian Church, that heavy blows should be struck against it by minds outside of it and intellectually hostile to it. Self-love, prejudice and vanity always make self-reform difficult. This wish of the poet, that

> Some one could the giftie gie us
> To see ourselves as others see us!

points out not only a weakness of an individual, but of a Church or a government. A despotism or a monarchy never doubts itself. It is necessary for some outside man, some Republican Kossuth or Patrick Henry, to spring the first doubt. So with the Church universal. Blinded by self-love, it has had to accept of reform at the hands of those standing outside of its atmosphere of mutual admiration. The Calvinistic faith could indeed reform the Armenian, and the Armenian the Calvanistic, and so on, until each sect had pruned away something from its neighbor's folly; but beyond this slight work there is a vast region in which all the denominations sat down together in a deep and mutual admiration, fatal to all sense of fault and to all hope of reform. It is necessary in these hours that blows should come from parties outside of itself.

All the Christian Church held to the justice of persecution even to the death. From Rome to Geneva and Edinburg, the stake and the gag-law were as universal as the Ten Commandments. In this awful condition of things, it was only a kind Providence that turned the French infidels loose into that field, dripping with the blood of the innocent Huguenot, and Covenanter, and Catholic. So the Church once sustained such relarions to slavery that light could not dawn upon it out of its own horizon, but was poured upon it by a free-thinking world moving in an orbit beyond the realm of the sanctuary. The relation of the Church to science and to woman awaits also a schooling from her enemies, and while it will never accept the whole argument of scientists, nor the whole declaration of woman's rights, as set forth by Mr. Mill and his school, yet by these outside voices it will be led into some new world of truth, brighter with the glory of both man and God.

There was another feature in the character of Mr. Mill that illustrates a cardinal idea of Christianity. You know the Bible is full of the idea that the soul is the chief thing. The Bible is the book of the soul. Christ came in the name of the soul. He himself had no property, no office, no empire, no equipage, no retinue, because he came in the name of the mind divine and immortal. The New Testament is the grandest delineation of the soul's greatness that ever came to earth through the lips of men. If you read the pages of profane history, you read of wars, armies, palaces, diadems, royal families. But, opening the New Testament, you read only of the immortal spirit. Over each page the golden word "soul" might well be written. In all profane history, the last word is dust; but of the Testament, the last word is always immortality, be the writer John, or Paul, or the Savior.

If it were not for such men as Mr. Mill coming here and there in human life, we might fail to know what that thing called soul is. I do not know where, in the public men of our land, we can see so well the picture of human dignity swayed out of balance by a love of office and gold; disturbed by a storm of bad passions, our public men reveal the soul, not in its nobleness, but in some shape that begs for pity and forgiveness.

Our great men are all said to die disappointed and half broken-hearted, because they fail to catch a four-year bauble from the tumultuous crowd. To run for President, and then die in glory or in cloud, according to the counting of the votes, has become a brief history of one of our greatest men. It is a sad remembrance of Mr. Greeley and Mr. Chase, that their failure to reach a great office turned their days into a winter of discontent.

All over our land, it seems to be forgotten that a human soul may be something to which no office can add anything, and from which no political defeat can take anything away.

God has in no way connected human greatness with a ballot-box:

> The boast of heraldry, the pomp of power,
>   And all that rank and fortune e'er gave,
> Await alike the inevitable hour;
>   And paths of glory lead but to the grave.

From such a scene it is sweet to turn to a man who might have honored any office, but whom no office could have honored. Nothing lasting for four years could have added to a soul great before the four years and great afterwards. Mr. Mill would scarcely have known when an earthly honor came to his forehead, or when it departed. Like Marcus Aurelius, whose laurels of virtue were greater than the throne of the Roman Empire, Mr. Mill's own forehead was nobler in itself than it could have been rendered by all the political wreaths of his generation.

True greatness never reveals nor cherishes much ambition, for the gift of mind and the possession of a profound character leave little for the soul to wish or for earth to confer. Hence in the blessed life of the Savior we perceive no trace of popular ambition, but everywhere simple greatness of spirit, as if that were the supreme destiny of rational being.

Oh, what an era would begin in our land if, instead of waiting for something outside of self to come to us and honor us, our citizens should unfold the glory within them as a flower sends forth beauty and perfume from its own opening heart!

Let me ask you now to come to one more point where Mr. Mill illustrated a truth that belongs by adoption to the family of religious ideas. The Catholic Church makes it a sacrament; the Protestant churches little less than that. But let the ceremony be considered civil or religious, the relation itself is all inwoven with the past and future of Christianity. There is no debate so loud and so apparently disgraceful as that now filling the civilized world over the nature and obligations of the marriage relation. It seems now to have been the good fortune of Mr. Mill to unfold by example this great form of friendship that was established in earth's first paradise. After the Greek and Roman picture in which the wife was a semi-slave, after the French and American picture in which the wife is an inferior or a creature of fashion, it leads us up to the old ideal of God when we behold the wife of a Stuart Mill to have been the perfect equal of him in education, in dignity, and in liberty. By educating our youth along difficult paths, man seeks to hold converse with man. He talks the highest thoughts to his brother, the humbler at his home. To this difference of education there is added the influence of the possession of power and authority held by man for thousands of years. Separated by long-cultivated vanity and long-assumed authority on the one side, and by difference of studies on both sides, and bound only by a transient sentiment called romance, the marriage bond of to-day stands exposed to constant peril of unhappiness or separation. It is a structure moved from its base. But in these two souls now gone from this shore we behold marriage triumphing in an education exactly parallel, and in a companionship that extended all through the divine spirit of each. It was a partnership of mind, a vast friendship and vast love mingled as an interweaving of intellect, and sentiment, and equality.

Before the spectacle of such a friendship all the modern discourse about the bondage of marriage appears as a madness. That flood of platform eloquence that rising in our Atlantic border has spread Westward as the Black Death that once spread out from Asia, seems to roll back from this tomb as though God stood there, saying, "Thus far and no farther."

These two studied the same works and alternated with each other in writing for the Reviews and in the deep work upon human liberty.

With these two souls before us, all the modern words about affinities, in the recent sense of that term, come to us as from a world of mingled vice and brutism, and leave us rapt in the admiration of an affinity of mind, of spirit, of purity, of immortality.

It may be that not many can reach such a vast, faultless friendship; but there it stands, the only ideal worthy of veneration or pursuit.

Of this marriage, divorce forms no more an element than it forms an element in the father's or mother's love for her child. The mother demands no exchange. There is no romance that may transfer her love from her child to that of some foreign home. This friendship is baffled only by death. Marriage is just such an imperishable, unalterable thing.

When one of our leading citizens, a few weeks since, wrung his hands in agony upon the banks of the river while his only son was dying beneath the waves, when the eye could not see him nor the hand help, we beheld in that scene a friendship that nothing but death could terminate. The only divorce of a father's love for his son is death.

While the tears of Stuart Mill were falling over the tomb of his unrivaled wife, the civilized world perceived that the marriage designed of God is one that nothing but the grave can end, and then by a profound sorrow.

But there is no perfection upon these shores. And now we come to the shadow that falls across this grave by day and night. That Mr. Mill did not accept the orthodox creed, is not what a liberal world need regret the most, but that he revealed little of the religious sentiment and hope is what we must confess to be a shadow upon his memory.

His career verifies what I have said here so often that it has become, I fear, wearisome to you, that the intellect alone does not lead to a Savior or a God in the religious sense. Mr. Mill, like Locke and Buckle, Darwin and Tyndall, so idolized the rational faculty, so idolized the visible, the tangible, and the immediate, that the sentiments seem to have perished by neglect.

When the human mind will go no farther than it can see clearly, it cannot go far from its cradle. It argues little against the central truths of Christianity that these great brain powers have rejected their claims, for they have gone further, and have, for the most part, dealt with deism itself just as with Christianity. Their hearts do not fail of Christianity, but of all religion.

This phenomenon of thousands of practical philosophers parting with religion does not teach me that the religious world is a fable, but does teach me that there are sentiments in the heart which, if slighted, will convert the earth into a laboratory, and death and love and wisdom and virtue all intoust.

Victor Cousin, of France, was the rival of Stuart Mill in wisdom, in genius, in intellect; and so Guizot. These three were similar and strikingly great. But the two latter possessed the power of sentiment. That golden atmosphere of love and hope that hangs around religion enveloped Victor Cousin in its life-giving folds. Setting out from the same points of thought, Cousin always came up to God and Heaven, and Mr. Mill to the practical of this life; to the happiness of man here, and then paused. Oh, what a deep mystery of human life is here:

From the same father's side,
  From the same mother's knee,
One journeys to a gloomy tide,—
  One to a peaceful sea.

And Cousin and Guizot teach us that there is no mental greatness too large for religion. That religion depends upon the world's credulity; but they teach us, even beside the grave of the lamented Mill, that religious sentiment is a divine part of human character, and ought to make its sunlight play in every bosom; and that the more gifted the genius the sweeter and more divine may be its colors in the soul's horizon.

THE CHARGES PREFERRED AGAINST DAVID SWING

BEFORE THE PRESBYTERY OF CHICAGO.

THE NOTIFICATION.

To the Reverend, the Presbytery of Chicago, in session in the Third Presbyterian Church, in the City of Chicago:

DEAR BRETHREN: In the month of August, 1873, I published in the *Interior* an editorial review of Professor Swing's sermon on "Old Testament Inspiration." It was written in the spirit of kindness, with no thought of controversy, and with no idea that it would lead to a judicial inquiry. To the discussion between Professor Swing and myself I need not refer, except to say that it was the occasion of a careful examination of his theological views as they appear in his writings. I have adverted to some of these views, as you are aware, in the columns of the *Interior*. Indeed, fidelity to the church of which I am a minister required me to do so. It would have given me great pleasure, as I know it would have been a great satisfaction to many others of his ministerial brethren, had this discussion resulted in a vindication of Professor Swing from any imputation of heresy, and in showing that he is a sincere believer in the doctrinal system of that church in which he has been so honored and loved; and, since this is not the case, it would have been more in accord with my feelings if some older member of the Presbytery could have assumed the responsibility of bringing the erroneous views of Professor Swing to your notice.

Circumstances, however, have combined to impose this painful task on me. Permit me, therefore, to call your attention to the accompanying charges, with their specifications, which I ask leave to prosecute at your bar.

Praying that the great Head of the Church may guide us in the solemn duties which will devolve upon us as a court of Jesus Christ, I am, very sincerely yours in the bonds of the gospel,

FRANCIS L. PATTON.

CHICAGO, April 13, 1874.

CHARGE FIRST.

The Rev. David Swing, being a minister of the Presbyterian Church in the United States of America, and a member of the Presbytery of Chicago, has not been zealous and faithful in maintaining the truths of the gospel; and has not been faithful and diligent in the exercise of the public duties of his office as such minister.

Specification First.—He is in the habit of using equivocal language in respect to fundamental doctrines, to the manifest injury of his reputation as a Christian minister, and to the injury of the cause of Christ: that is to say, in sundry sermons printed in the *Chicago Pulpit*, and in sundry other sermons printed in the *Alliance* newspaper, and also in sundry other sermons printed in a volume entitled "Truths for To-Day," said sermons all purporting to have been preached by him, the references to one or more of the following doctrines, to-wit: the person of our Lord, regeneration, salvation by Christ, eternal punishment, the personality of the Spirit, the Trinity, and the fall of man, are expressed in vague and ambiguous language; that said references admit easily of construction in accordance with the theology of the Unitarian denomination; that they contain no distinct and unequivocal affirmations of these doctrines as they are held by all evangelical churches.

Specification Second.—That the effect of these vague and ambiguous statements has been to cause grave doubts to be entertained by some of Mr. Swing's ministerial brethren respecting his position in relation to the aforesaid doctrines; that leading Unitarian ministers, to-wit: Rev. R. Laird Collier and Rev. Minot J. Savage, have affirmed that his preaching is substantially Unitarian; that Mr. Swing, knowing that he is claimed by Unitarians as in substantial accord with them, and of the doubts existing as aforesaid, and moreover, having his attention called in private interviews to the ambiguity and vagueness of his phraseology, has neglected to preach the doctrine of our Lord's Deity, the doctrine of the Trinity, of Justification by Faith alone, and of the eternal punishment of the wicked.

Specification Third.—He has manifested a culpable disregard of the essential doctrines of Christianity by giving the weight of his influence to the Unitarian denomination, and by the unworthy and extravagant laudation in the pulpit, and through the press, of one who is known not to have believed in the Christian religion; that is to say, that some time in the past winter, and during successive days, he was advertised to lecture in the city of Chicago in aid of a Unitarian chapel, and that he did lecture in aid of said chapel, and in doing so aided in the promulgation of the heresy which denies the Deity of our blessed Lord; that in an article written by him, and published over his name in the periodical called the *Lakeside Monthly*, bearing date October, 1873, and entitled "The Chicago of the Christian," a passage occurs, which, taken in its plain and obvious sense, teaches that Robert Collyer, a Unitarian minister, and Robert Patterson, a Presbyterian minister, preach substantially the same gospel; that the gospel, meaning the Christian religion, is mutable, and may be modified by circumstances of time and place; that the "local gospel," meaning the gospel of Chicago, is a "mode of virtue" rather than a "jumble of doctrines;" and moreover, that on the Sabbath following the death of John Stuart Mill, a well-known Atheist, Mr. Swing preached a sermon in reference to Mr. Mill, the natural effect of which would be to mislead and injure his hearers by producing in them a false charity for fundamental error.

Specification Fourth.—In the sermons aforesaid, language is employed which is derogatory to the standards of the Presbyterian Church, or to one or more of the doctrines of said church, and which is calculated to foster indifference to truth, and to produce contempt for the doctrines of our church; that is to say, that he has at sundry times spoken disparagingly of the doctrine of the Trinity, Predestination, the Person of Christ, Baptism, the Christian Ministry, and Vicarious Sacrifice; that by insinuation, ridicule, irony, and misrepresentation he has referred to the doctrines of our church in such a way as to show that he does not value them; and that by placing in juxtaposition true doctrines and false minor points in theology and cardinal doctrines of evangelical religion, he has treated some of the most precious doctrines of our religion with contempt. The reference is particularly to sermons entitled "Soul Culture," "St. Paul and the Golden Age," "Salvation and Morality," "Value of Yesterday," "Influence of Democracy on Christian Doctrine," "Variation of Moral Motive," "A Religion of Words," all published in the *Chicago Pulpit*, and to "Religious Toleration," "Christianity and Dogma," "Faith," "The Great Debate," "Christianity as a Civilization," published in "Truths for To-Day," and in the sermons entitled "The Decline of Vice," "Christianity a Life," and a "Missionary Religion," published in the *Alliance* newspaper. The following passage illustrates the allegation: "Over the idea that two and two make four no blood has been shed; but over the insinuation that three may be one, or one three, there has often been a demand for external influence to brace up for the work the frail logical faculty. It is probable that no man has ever been put to death for heresy regarding the Sermon on the Mount. Its declarations demand no tortures to aid human faith; but when a church comes along with its 'legitimacy,' or with its Five Points, or with its Prayer Book, or its Infant Baptism, or Eternal Procession of the Holy Ghost, then comes the demand for the rack and the stake to make up in terrorism what is wanting in evidence."

Specification Fifth.—Being a minister of the Presbyterian Church, and preaching regularly to the Fourth Presbyterian Church of this city, he has omitted to preach in his sermons the doctrines commonly known as evangelical — that is to say, in particular, he omits to preach or teach one or more of the doctrines indicated in the following statements of Scripture, namely: that Christ is a "propitiation for our sins," that we have "redemption through His blood," that we are "justified by faith," that "there is no other name under heaven given among men whereby we may be saved," that Jesus is "equal with God," and is "God manifest in the flesh," that "all Scripture is given by inspiration of God," and that "the wicked shall go away into everlasting punishment."

Specification Sixth.—He declares that the value of a doctrine is measured by the ability of men to verify it in their experience. In illustrating this statement he has spoken lightly of important doctrines of the Bible; that is to say, that in a sermon entitled "Christianity and Dogma," printed in the volume called "Truths for To-Day," the following and similar language is used: "The doctrines of Christianity are those which may be tried by the human heart." "The doctrine of the Trinity as formally stated cannot be experienced. Man has not the power to taste the oneness of three, nor the threeness of one, and see that it is 'good.'" "If you, my friend, are giving your daily thought to the facts of Christianity, and are standing bewildered to-day amid the statements of science and Genesis about earth or its swarms of life, recall the truth that your soul cannot taste any theory of man's origin—cannot experience the origin of man, whatever that origin may have been."

Specification Seventh.—In the sermons entitled respectively, "Old Testament Inspiration," and "The Value of Yesterday," published in the *Chicago Pulpit*, and in sermons entitled "Righteousness," "Faith," "The Great Debate," printed in "Truths for To-Day;" also, in the "Decline of Vice," printed in the *Alliance*, he has used language which, taken in its plain and obvious sense, inculcates a phase of the doctrine commonly known as "Evolution" or "Development;" that is to say, he uses the following and similar language: "Low idolatry of primitive man," meaning Adam. "The Bible has not made religion, but religion and righteousness have made the Bible. Christianity it not forced upon us—our own nature has forced it up out of the spirit's rich depths." "The Mosaic economy was nothing else but progress; earth had come to Polytheism, to Pantheism, to Fetichism. It was the Hebrew philosophy and its immediate result, Christianity, which swept away the iron Jupiter." "This multitude measures a great revelation of God above that day when earth possessed but one man or family, and that one without language, and without learning, and without virtue." "In the first human being God could no more display His perfections than a musician like Mozart could unfold his genius to an infant or to a South-Sea Islander." These passages conflict with the Confession of Faith, Chap. 8, Sec. 1; Chap. 7, Sec. 3, 4, 5; Chap. 4, Sec. 2.

Specification Eighth.—In a sermon entitled "Influence of Democracy on Christian Doctrine," published in the *Chicago Pulpit*, and preached April 20, 1873, he has made false and dangerous statements regarding the standards of faith and practice; that is to say, he uses the following and similar language: "When we come to moral ideas we are compelled to do without any standards." "You may, my friends, at your leisure seek and find further instances of the modification of Christian belief by the new surroundings of government. Christian customs will also be modified along with the creed." "In this casting off of old garments, it no more cheerfully throws away the inconceivable of Christianity than the inconceivable of Kant and Spinoza." "In this abandonment there is no charge of falsehood cast upon the old mysteries; they may or may not be true—there is only a passing them by as not being in a line of the current wish or taste—raiment for a past age, perhaps for a future, but not acceptable for the present."

Specification Ninth.—He has given his approval in the pulpit to the doctrine commonly known as Sabellianism, or a Modal Trinity, and has spoken slightingly of the doctrine of the Trinity, as taught in the standards of the Presbyterian Church (Confession of Faith, Chap. 2, Sec. 3); that is to say, in the volume "Truths for To-Day," he uses the following and similar language: "But the moment that He (Jesus) has uttered our text, that 'Those which man can subject to experience are the doctrines that be of God,' reason rises up and unites its voice with that of simple authority. The doctrines of Christianity are those which may be tried by the human heart." "The doctrine of the Trinity, as formally stated, cannot be experienced. Man has not the power to taste the threeness of one nor the oneness of three, and see that it is 'good.'" "Hence, Christianity bears readily the idea of three offices, and permits the one God to appear in Father, or in Son, or in Spirit."

Specification Tenth.—In the sermons entitled, respectively, "The Great Debate," and "Positive Religion," printed in the volume called "Truths for To-Day," false and dangerous statements are made respecting our knowledge regarding the Being and attributes of God: that is to say, that the following and similar language is used: "When Logic informs you and me that God is a law, or a widespread blind agency, let us not be deceived, for all it has done is to take away *our* God." "Perfect assurance is just as impossible to a free religionist or Atheist, as it is to the Christian. Remembering, therefore, that there is no moral idea of beauty or love or soul that may not be denied, and remembering, too that the assurance that there is a God is always logically equal to the opposite belief." "We know not what nor where is our God, our heaven." (Confession of Faith, Chap. 2, Sec. 1, and Chap. 2.)

Specification Eleventh.—In a sermon entitled "A Religion of Words," published in the *Chicago Pulpit*, and in the sermon entitled "Religious Toleration," he uses language in regard to the Sacrament of Baptism inconsistent with the doctrinal standards of the Presbyterian Church (see Confession of Faith, Chap. 28, Secs. 1, 2, 3, 4, and Chap. 28, Secs. 1, 5;) that is to say, he speaks flippantly of infant baptism, and, in the sermon above mentioned, uses the following words: "The nations await, with tears of past sorrow, a religion that shall indeed baptize men and children, either or both, but, counting this as only a beautiful form, shall take the souls of men into the atmosphere of Jesus," etc.

Specification Twelfth.—He has used language in respect to Penelope and Socrates which is unwarrantable and contrary to the teachings of the Confession of Faith, Chap. 10, Sec. 24; that is to say, in his sermon entitled "Soul-Culture," the following passage occurs: "There is no doubt the notorious Catherine II. held more truth and better truth than was known to all classic Greece—held to a belief in a Savior, of whose glory that gifted soul knew nought; yet, such the grandeur of soul above mind, that I doubt not that Queen Penelope, of the dark land, and the doubting Socrates have received at heaven's gate a sweeter welcome than greeted the ear of Russia's brilliant but false-lived Queen."

Specification Thirteenth.—In a sermon printed on or about 15th September, 1872, from Peter iii: 9, he made use of loose and unguarded language respecting the Providence of God.

Specification Fourteenth.—In a sermon preached at the installation of the Rev. Arthur Swazey, D. D., as pastor of the Ashland Avenue Presbyterian Church, Chicago, and previously preached about January, 1872, in Standard Hall, Chicago, he repudiated the idea of a call to the ministry, and taught that the office of the ministry, like the profession of law and medicine, is the natural outgrowth of circumstances; that is to say, he said in substance, that the merchant is called to his business, the lawyer to his profession, just as much as the minister to the duties of his office, and other statements contradicting the teachings of the Confession of Faith in Chap. xxv., Sec. 3, and Forms of Government, Chap. i. See Confession of Faith, Chap. xxx., Secs. 1 and 2. Confession of Faith, Chap. xxvii., Sec. 4; Chap. vii., Sec. 4; Chap. xxix., Sec. 3.

Specification Fifteenth.—He has made false and misleading statements respecting the Old Testament sacrifices; that is to say, that in the sermon entitled "A Religion of Words," he speaks of the aforesaid sacrifices as "gift worship," and uses the following and similar language: "Gifts to the Deity were the infant creepings of religion; the shadow of a coming reality, the manifesting of an incipient love that did not know how to express itself. Not knowing that what God most wished, was a pure heart in His children, they loaded His temples with their jewels and raiment, and His altars with their lambs." See Confession of Faith: Chap. vii., Sec. 5; Chap. viii., Sec. 4; Chap. xiv., Sec. 3. Larger Catechism, Q. 34.

Specification Sixteenth.—In the sermon aforesaid, religion is represented in the form of a mysticism, which undervalues the evidences of revealed religion, and is indifferent to the distinguishing doctrines of Christianity; that is to say, that in the sermon preached on the occasion of the death of John Stuart Mill, above referred to, and in the sermon called "Positive Religion," printed in "Truths for To-day;" also, in the sermon entitled "The Decline of Vice," printed in the *Alliance* newspaper; and in the volume called "Truths for To-day," the following and similar language occurs: "That Mr. Mill did not accept the orthodox creed is not what a liberal world need regret the most, but that he revealed little of the religious sentiment and hope is we must confess to be a shadow upon his memory." "Victor Cousin of France was the rival of Stuart Mill in wisdom, in genius, in intellect; and so Guizot. These three were similar and strikingly great. But the two latter possessed the power of sentiment. That golden atmosphere of love and hope, that hangs around religion, enveloped Victor Cousin in its life-giving folds. Setting out from the same points of thought, Cousin always came up to God and heaven, and Mr. Mill to the practical of this life; to the happiness of man here, and then paused."

Specification Seventeenth.—In the sermons aforesaid, he employs the words used to indicate the doctrines of the Bible in an unscriptural sense, and in a sense different from that in which they are used by the Evangelical churches in general, and the Presbyterian Church in particular; that is to say, that he so uses such words as "regeneration," "conversion," "repentance," "Divine," "justification," "new heart," "salvation," "Savior."

Specification Eighteenth.—He, in effect, denies the judicial nature of the condemnation of the lost, as taught in the Confession of Faith, Chap. iv., Sec. 4, Chap. xxxiii. Shorter Catechism, q. xix., q. 84; that is to say, in the sermon entitled "Faith, and Christianity, and Dogma," printed in the volume called "Truths for To-Day," he uses the following and similar language: "The least trace of infidelity lessons the activity; unbelief brings all to a halt, and damns the soul, not by arbitrary decree, but by actually arresting the best flow of its life. Unbelief is not an arbitrary but a natural damnation."

Specification Nineteenth.—He teaches that faith saves, because it leads to holy life; that salvation by faith is not peculiar to Christianity; that salvation is a matter of degree, and that the supremacy of faith in salvation arises out of the fact that it goes further than other Christian graces towards making men holy, that is to say, in the sermons entitled "Faith," printed in the volume called "Truths for To-day," the following and similar language occurs: "Faith in Christ is a rich soil out of which righteousness is a gorgeous bloom." "If there were enough truth—truth of morals and redemption in the Mohammedan or Budhist system to save the soul—faith would be the law of salvation within these systems." "Salvation by faith is not a creation or invention of the New Testament, but is a law that has pushed its way up into the New Testament from the realm without." "No other grace could so save the soul. Charity may do much. It softens the heart, and drags along a train of virtues; but it is limited by the horizon of this life. Voltaire and Paine were both beautiful in charity toward the poor, but that virtue seems inadequate; and, of the highest form of charity, a religious faith is the best cause, and hence charity must take the place, not of a leader, but of one that is led. Even penitence is a poor 'saving grace,' compared with faith." See Confession of Faith, Chaps. xi., xvi.

Specification Twentieth.—He teaches that men are saved by works; that is to say, in the sermons entitled "Good Works," "The Value of Yesterday," "A religion of Words," and other sermons, the following and similar language occurs: "There is nothing society so much needs to-day as not Divine righteousness but human righteousness." "Heaven is a height to which men climb on the deeds of this life." "Coming to the grave, he can only look forward with joy who can sweetly look back." "The good deeds of yesterday, the good deeds of to-day, the perfected goodness of to-morrow, a deep love for man, a consciousness of the presence of God, will fill the whole place with a nobleness and happiness to which earth has thus far been willingly a stranger. This will be a salvation, and Christ will be a salvation?" [Confession of Faith, Chap. xi., Sec. 14.]

Specification Twenty-first.—He denies the doctrine of Justification by Faith, as held by the Reformed Churches, and taught in the Westminster Confession of Faith; Chap. 9, that is to say, in the sermon entitled "Good Works," he uses the following and similar language: "Works, that is, results—a new life—are the destiny of faith, the reason of its wonderful play of light on the religious horizon. Faith, as a belief and a friendship, is good, so far as it bears the soul to this moral perfection."

Specification Twenty-second.—He misrepresents the doctrinal views of those who believe in Justification by Faith alone, by using language which is calculated to produce the impression that those who hold the doctrine aforesaid divorce faith from morals, and believe that men may be saved by an intellectual assent to a creed without regard to personal character.

Specification Twenty-third.—He has spoken of the Bible, or portions thereof, in terms which involve a denial of its plenary inspiration as held in the Presbyterian Church and taught in the Confession of Faith, Chapter i. and also in the following passages of Scripture, (2 Tim. iii: 16; Acts i: 16-20,) that is to say, in a sermon entitled "Old Testament Inspiration," and in sundry articles written by him and printed in the *Interior* newspaper, he refers to the 109th Psalm as a "battle-song," as the "good of an hour," "a revenge;" and in an article printed in the *Interior* Sept. 18, 1873, he uses the following and similar language: "The prominence given to the 109th Psalm in my remarks arises only from the fact that it has long been a public test of the value of any given theory of inspiration. This is one of the places at which the rational world asks us to pause and apply our abundant and boastful words. Most of the young men, even in the Presbyterian Church, know what the historian Froude, said of this psalm a few years since; 'Those who accept the 109th Psalm as the word of God, are already far on their way toward *auto-da-fes* and massacres of St. Bartholomew,' and while they may, for a time, reject these words, they will soon demand a theory of inspiration very different from the indefinite admiration of the past."

Specification Twenty-fourth.—He has spoken of the Bible, or portions thereof, in terms which involve a denial of its infallibility, and which tend to shake the confidenee of men in its divine authority,—as taught in Confession of Faith, Chap. i., that is to say, in the sermon on "Old Testament Inspiration," the following passages occur: "There is, it seems to me, no other conceivable method of treating the Old Testament than that found in the word *ecleticism*. We must seek out its permanent truths, follow its central ideas, and love them the more because they were eliminated from the barbaric ages with so much sorrow and bloodshed." Moreover, in the article in the *Interior* above mentioned, he says that "Christ declared the Ten Commandments defective;" also, in the article written by him and printed in the *Interior*, Sept. 4, 1873, he speaks of "battles"—meaning the battles of the Israelites—engaged in with the approval and by the command of Jehovah, "that surpassed in cruelty those of Julius Cæsar." He also teaches that the Mosaic legislation was cruel and unjust, and uses the following and similar language: "If David's personal character had been preceded by generations which dripped in blood, by generations which punished over thirty forms of offenses with death, by generations which slew women and children, by generations which punished impurity by a fine of one animal from the flock; and, if reared in such an atmosphere, David sent Uriah to the front and thus secured Uriah's beauteous wife, one certainly should not attribute this immortality to any lack of revelation, indeed, but rather to an absence of that quality of revelation found afterwards in the morals of Jesus." Moreover, in an article written by him and printed in the periodical known as the "Sunday School Teacher," and bearing date July, 1873, he uses the following and similar language. And, moreover, in a sermon entitled "St. John," printed in the volume called "Truths for To-Day," he uses the following and similar language: "There are no prophecies of literal events in the Apocalypse any more than there is in Tasso, or Tennyson, or Whittier." * * * "For us to inquire the meaning of the several seals, and to inquire whether Rome be not the 'Babylon,' would be for us to seek the 'Deserted Village' of Goldsmith or the 'Beulah Land' of John Bunyan."

The foregoing charge with its specifications may be proved by the printed sermons and articles of Mr. Swing, as above mentioned, and by the testimony of the following witnesses:

Oliver H. Lee, Horace A. Hurlburt, William C. Gray, Charles M. Howe, Leonard Swett, William C. Ewing, Mr. McClurg (of Jansen & McClurg), Messrs. Carpenter and Sheldon, the Rev. W. C. Young, the Rev. J. B. McClure, the Rev. R. K. Wharton, the Rev. C. L. Thompson, the Rev. R. Laird Collier, the Rev. J. Minot Savage, C. O. Waters, the Rev. Arthur Swazey, D. D., F. A. Riddle, the Rev. R. W. Patterson, D. D., A. D. Pence, John McLandburg, the Rev. Robert Collyer, Henry G. Miller, William C. Goudy, the Rev. J. H. Trowbridge.

CHARGE SECOND.

The Rev. David Swing, being a minister of the Presbyterian Church in the United States of America, and a member of the Presbytery of Chicago, does not sincerely receive and adopt the Confession of Faith of this Church as containing the system of doctrine taught in the Holy Scriptures.

Specification First.--Since he began to minister to the Fourth Presbyterian Church he has declared to the Rev. Robert Laird Collier, a Unitarian minister in charge of the Church of the Messiah, in Chicago, in substance, that he agreed with him, Collier, in his theological views, but thought it best to remain as he was for the time, as he could thereby accomplish more good for the cause.

Specification Second.—He does not accept and believe doctrines contained in the Confession of Faith, viz.: the doctrines commonly known as predestination, the Perseverance of the Saints, and Depravity.

Specification Third.—That he has declared, in a letter to George A. Shufeldt, Esq., about the year 1867, that he had long before that time abandoned three of the five points of Calvinism affirmed by the Synod of Dort, naming the three, meaning three of the doctrines adopted and taught in the Confession of Faith.

Specification Fourth.—That in a sermon delivered in the Fourth Presbyterian Church, April 12, 1874, he made statements which, by fair implication, involve a disbelief in one or more of the leading doctrines of Confession of Faith, to-wit: Of Election, Perseverance, Original Sin, the Vicarious Sacrifice of Christ, the Trinity, and the Deity of Christ, that is to say, he uses the following and similar language:

"After the hundred-year experiment, there is no probability that any missionary gold will be exhausted upon any indoctrination of the heathen world in denominational ideas, for the tendency of the present is to abandon sectarian ideas at home; hence their will be little disposition to inculcate abroad doctrines which are rapidly dying by our own firesides."

"The Church of England joins with the dissenting churches in India as a fact, and cares little for the apostolic succession in a land where the Brahmin can so far outdo it in the quantity or absurdity of holy teachings and holy pedigrees. And there the Calvinist conceals his five points, for the crowd of Indian philosophers can always propose ten points far more obscure, and thus all the Protestant sects approach the whole Pagan world with the Gospel reduced to its simplest expression. Blessed era it will be when we shall be as fully ashamed in America of the things that divide us as we are when our feet touch India or Japan."

"Can it be possible that it requires home training, that is, local and youthful prejudice, to enable us to see the immense worth of our dogmas, and that, approaching foreigners not fully drilled in the sectarian method and tactics, we fear their smile of unbelief or derision? It is ominous if, having a score or so of peculiar ideas, we should all get together and agree to say little about them to this Chinaman and that Brahmin. Such a condition of things would seem to indicate one more step along this path, an agreement to say little about these differences to persons not pagans, and not upon foreign shores.

"We have come to-day to a survey of Christianity in its truest significance, and hence in its wanderings about from race to race, from island to continent, from river to sea, we may learn what are its most essential parts. A student shutting himself up in his room may, from the Bible, elaborate a perfect system which shall omit nothing regarding the human will or the mode and quality of everything, but the world in actual experiment may not need, nor even faintly appreciate, one-tenth part of this closet-made system."

The specifications contained under Charge 1 are relied on as contained under and in support of Charge 2, the same as if repeated, excepting the sixth, tenth, and sixteenth.

The foregoing charge with its specifications may be proved by the printed writings of Mr. Swing, as above referred to, and by the testimony of the following writers: Robert Laird Collier, George A. Shufeldt, and also of the witnesses named in Charge 1.

DAVID SWING'S TRIAL.

The Chicago Presbytery met in the lecture room of the First Presbyterian Church, corner of Twenty-First street and Indiana avenue, at half-past 10 o'clock, on Monday morning, May 4, 1874, for the purpose of trying Prof. Swing, upon the charges of heresy and unfaithfulness, preferred against him by the Rev. Dr. Patton. The Moderator, the Rev. Arthur Mitchell, occupied the chair, and there were present, the Revs. Dr. R. W. Patterson, L. J. Halsey, A. Swazey F. L. Patton, W. C. Young, A. H. Dean, J. V. Downs, J. M. Fairs, W. M. Blackham, E. W. Barrett, G. C. Meyers, W. Forsythe, W. J. Wood, John Covert, E. R. Davis, E. L. Hurd, W. F. Browne, E. Scofield, J. B. McClure, J. Munroe Gibson, J. H. Taylor, Joseph H. Burns, A. Mitchell, J. H. Trowbridge, J. H. Walker, M. M. Wakeman, J. McLeod, W. R. Downs, J. T. Matthews, P. Cardin, C. L. Thompson, C. Wisner, D. J. Burrell, A. E. Kittredge, Glen Wood, L. H. Reid, Jacob Post, E. H. Curtis, David Swing, D. S. Johnson, William Broteston, James Harrison, R. K. Wharter.

The roll of churches and their lay representatives was next called, and the following responded: First Church, J. A. Otis; Second Church, J. S. Gould; Third Church, J. M. Horton; Fourth Church, O. H. Lee; Fifth Church, Elijah Smith; Eighth Church, J. E. Fay; Jefferson Avenue Church, Tuthill King; Grace Church, George H. Frost; Ashland Avenue Church, F. A. Riddle; Westminster Church, J. D. Wallace; Evanston Church, A. L. Winne; Hyde Park Church, H. A. Hopkins; Highland Park Church, S. B. Williams; Lake Forest Church, D. R. Holt; Manteno Church, C. A. Spring; Homewood Church, J. Caldwell; Joliet Central Church, R. E. Barber; Maywood Church, J. H. Hurlburt; Reunion Church, A. H. Merrill; Englewood Church, A. Drysdale; Dunton Church, W. H. Dunton; Fullerton Avenue Church, Morton Lewis; Ninth Church, George H. Leonard; Joliet First Church, W. P. Caton; Wilmington Church, William Hart; Peotone Church, Henry Marsdon. In addition to these, there are about 200 spectators, principally ladies, who occupied seats outside the Presbyters, the latter sitting in the body of a semicircle.

The proceedings were opened by spending a few moments in silent prayer, and then the Moderator asked God that the spirit of a true Christian brotherhood might be spread over the assembly, that he would be with them, and guide them to just conclusions.

DAVID SWING'S DECLARATION.

Prof. Swing then approached the Moderator's seat, and as he stepped on the platform, the audience applauded loudly.

The Moderator—The Moderator must call the audience to order. I think that they will appreciate that, in an assembly of this kind, in which we are sitting in a judicial capacity, it is entirely inappropriate for members of the Judicatory, and certainly still more for those who are not, to indulge in any expression of feeling of this kind. I hope silence will be observed in the future.

Prof. Swing—I wish to state, Mr. Moderator, that the form in which I shall bring my case forward is one about which I have great doubt, as I have had no conferences, and feel that I can only read my statement by a sort of charity on the part of the accuser.

The Professor then read as follows:

To the Members of the Chicago Presbytery:

Called upon in the outset of these proceedings to enter my plea to the charges and specifications presented by Francis L. Patton, I beg permission to submit the following: I object to the charges as too vague, and as embracing no important offense, yet, not wishing to raise any technical objections, I enter the plea of "Not guilty." I admit the extracts from sermons and writings, but I would ask the Presbytery to consider the entire essay or whole discourses from which the extracts are made. I avow myself to be what, before the late union, was styled a New School Presbyterian, and deny myself to have come into conflict with any of the Evangelical Calvanistic doctrines of the denomination with which I am connected, and I beg permission to enter as a part of my plea the following statements: 1. Regarding my relations to the Liberal Churches. 2. Regarding my relation with the Presbyterian Church. Of these I shall speak in their order.

By way of explaining the quantity of the public offense, I will state that of fifteen lectures delivered in this city for benevolent purposes, all but two were on behalf of the Evangelical Churches, and, in all cases but one, remuneration was declined. Hence the spirit that prompted such lectures must have been not any marked partiality for the so-called liberal societies. This much as to the quantity of the alleged offense. Upon the quality of the conduct, I would submit the following observations:

1. There is no valuable theory of life except that of "Good will toward all men." It is only upon the basis of a wide friendship any one can live well the few years of this existence, and, hence, to decline to lecture on behalf of a Unitarian chapel would be doing more harm to the mutual good will upon which society is founded than it would do good to an orthodox theology, or harm to a liberal creed.

2. If the object of the Evangelical pulpit is to promulge its better truth, it can do so only so far as its ministry reveal a deep friendship toward all mankind, and so far as they unfurl the banner of their own love, while they are presuming to speak of the impartial love of their Divine Master. There remains no longer any power of authority in the pulpit. The time when the civil police drove a halting sinner into the true Church has disappeared, and the modern pulpit must communicate its ideas along the chords of friendship, and he will persuade the most men whose heart can gather up the largest and most diverse multitude into the grasp of his pure affections.

3. But let us come now to the grandest reason why a Presbyterian may express in many ways a kind regard for these so-called Liberal sects. The sin of the "lecture" as charged, must be based upon the assumption that the Unitarian sects are outcasts from God, having no hope in the life to come. The names of Channing, and Elliott, and Huntington and Peabody, in the pulpits of that sect, and the Christ-like lives of thousands in the congregations of that denomination, utterly exclude from my mind and my heart the most remote idea that in showing that brotherhood any kindness, I am offering indirect approval to persons outside the pale of the Christian religion and hope. The idea that these brethren are doomed to wrath beyond the tomb, I wholly repudiate. It is, indeed, my conviction that they do not hold as correct a version of the Gospel as that announced by the Evangelical Alliance a few years ago, yet I am just as certain that the blessed Lord does not bestow his forgiveness and grace upon the mind that possesses the most accurate information, but upon the heart that loves and trusts Him. It is possible that the venerable Dr. Hodge, of Princeton, holds a more truthful view of Jesus than may be held by the distinguished Peabody, who has just lectured from his Unitarian standpoint before the Calvinists in the Union Theological Seminary, but we can point to nothing in the Bible that would indicate that Heaven is to be given to only the one of these two giants, who may possess a clearer apprehension of the truth. It may be assumed that God grants the world salvation only on account of the expiatory atonement made by a Redeemer, but that God will grant this

salvation to only those who fully apprehend this fact, is an idea not to be entertained for an instant, for this would give Heaven only to philosophers, and, indeed, only to those of this small class who shall have made no intellectual mistake. Looking upon the multitudes who need this salvation, and seeing that they are composed of common men, women and children, who know nothing of the distinctions of formal theology, we cannot but conclude that paradise is not to be a reward of scholarship, but of a loving, obedient faith in Jesus Christ.

When we remember these things, and recall that Dr. Isaac Watts was accused of being a Unitarian, so difficult often is it to perceive the dividing line, we cannot for a moment place these persons called Unitarians outside the great and generous love of the Savior. I stand ready, therefore, at all times to express toward these sects a friendship not only human, and wise, and social, but also Christian.

The harmony existing between all these brethren and myself is not a harmony of views in the mind, but a harmony of love in the soul. They each and all know that I differ widely from them, but this they and I know: that only the most gentlemanly treatment in public and private will we all receive always from each other. Much as I love Presbyterianism, a love inherited from all my ancestors, if on account of it, it were necessary for me to abate in the least my good will toward all sects, I should refuse to purchase the Presbyterian name at so dear a price.

The second point to be alluded to, was my relations to Presbyterianism. A distinction evidently exists between Presbyterianism as formulated in past times and Presbyterianism *actual*. A creed is only the highest wisdom of a particular time and place. Hence, as in States, there is always a quiet slipping away from old laws without any waiting for a formal repeal, as some of the old statutes of Connecticut are lying dead, not by any legal death, but by long emaciation and final utter neglect of friend and foe ; so in all formulated creeds, Catholic or Protestant, there is a gradual, but constant, decay of some article or word which was once promulged amid great pomp and circumstance. And yet, no Church is willing to confess its past folly and repeal the injurious or untrue. All, Catholic and Protestant, simply agree to remain silent.

In the Presbyterian Confession of Faith there are about 200 formulas of truth, or supposed truth. It is a wonderful argument in favor of this compendium that not one-tenth of these have been found false to the Bible or false to the welfare of society. To designate these 200 as Calvinism is a gross injustice, for they are almost all only valuable truths, common to all churches, and gathered up from the sacred page.

But from a few statements out of this large number the *actual* Presbyterian Church has quietly passed away. Conventions cannot be called every few years to amend or repeal some one article. It would entail endless debate and expense, and perhaps promote wide discord thus to call from time to time a new Westminster Assembly. As a Christian world avoids a revision of the translation of the Bible because of the tumult such a new version would probably create among the sects, so each particular Church postpones as long as possible any formal modification of its historic statements of doctrines. But meanwhile individual minds cannot be slaves; they cannot suspend the use of their judgment and best common sense. Hence, unable to revoke any dangerous idea by law, the Presbyterian Church permits its clergy to distinguish *actual* from the Church *historic*. To the Presbyterian Church actual I have thus far devoted my life, giving it what I possess of mind and heart.

Chief among the doctrines which our church has passed by as being incorrect, or else an overdevelopment of Scriptural ideas, are all those formulas which look toward a dark fatalism or which destroy the human will, or indicate the damnation of some infant, or that God, for His own glory, foreordained a vast majority of the race to everlasting death. It has been my good or bad fortune to speak in public, and in private to a large number of persons hostile to our church, and in nearly all cases I have found their hostility based upon the doctrines indicated above, and in all ways, I have declared to them that the Presbyterian Church had left behind those doctrines, and that her religion was simply evangelical, and not, *par excellence*, the religion of despair. In my peculiar ministry a simple silence has not been sufficient. I have, therefore, at many times declared our denomination to be simply a church of the common evangelical doctrines.

Besides the formulas of its books, our church has suffered more than pen can record from the wild utterances of some of its great names, and from these it has been my frequent duty to try to separate her fair and sweeter present. There were ages when mothers wailed in awful agony over a dead infant because they had been taught that children "not a span long" were suffering on the hot floor of hell, and that each new-born infant was only a "lump of perdition;" and, under the awful lashing of these thoughts, mothers used to baptize their *dead-born* little ones, piteously beseeching God to ante-date the sacred rite. In the midst of this wail of infants damned, Luther himself says: "God pleaseth you when He crowns the unworthy; He ought not to displease you when He damns the innocent."

Against the doctrine of fatalism, as implied in the perfect

independence of God's decree as to all human con ct, against the ultra form of human inability it has been my constant duty, as it seemed, to protest, and thus defend our church from the influence of ideas so repudiated by modern thought. An eminent churchman, perhaps Luther, said, "All things take place by the eternal and invariable will of God, who blasts and shatters in pieces the freedom of the will."

Next to the baneful Calvanistic estimate of the will, comes the overstatement of the idea of salvation by faith all along through the Presbyterian history. Said Luther, "You see how rich is the Christian. Even if he would, he could not destroy his salvation by any sins, however grievous, unless he refuse to believe." "Be thou a sinner and sin boldly, still more *boldly believe*. From Christ no sin shall separate, though a thousand thousand times a day we should commit fornication and murder." In my ministry I have toiled the harder to unite faith and holiness, because of this dreadful page of history written down against the Calvinistic branches of the Protestant Church.

Next to the injury the Presbyterian Church has sustained from its errors as above mentioned, it has become a source of actual infidelity by its terrific doctrine of hell. Even to the day of Edwards, and since, the pictures of perdition have been such as at first, indeed, to frighten the multitude, but such as afterward to destroy the idea of God. Look where men might, it was perdition to all but his sect, and, to look upon other sects in the pains of hell, was to form a part of the happiness of the blessed. The faggot, the rack, and the boiling oil were a resort of potentates, for, if God was so glorying in the torment of heretics just beyond, it was a small matter if the church tormented them slightly on this side the tomb. We need not disguise the fact, my brethren, that the dark side of Calvanism gave birth to infidelity in that age when the church was narrow in its love, broad only in its damnation. But permit me to quote from one who has not been arraigned for bad teaching, but whose words have just been published by the American Tract Society—Theodore Christlieb. He says: "It was the former century which prepared the way among ourselves for the prevalence of rationalism. Was it not the petrifaction of evangelical faith into dry forms of a dead orthodoxy? The sermons of that period were for the most part * * * about Crypto-Calvinists, Syncredists, Synergists, Majorists, Antinomians, Osiandrians, Weigelians, and Arminians. * * * At such a time, when a cold orthodoxy was almost everywhere substituted for living faith, when a slavish adherence to the church's standards was put in place of a free inquiry into the sense of Scripture, and a fresh bondage to the letter was introduced, it became a simple necessity for energetic minds like

Lessing to come to an open breach with traditional Protestantism. * * * Rationalism was right in contending for simple morality in opposition to a theoretic orthodoxy." "It must be confessed that the church theology of the last century was chiefly to blame for the general apostasy from the ancient faith which then began. From the middle of the eighteenth century to the end of the first third of the nineteenth, the chief authorities in pulpits and institutions of learning were promoters of rationalism. * * * For this spirit we theologians have only ourselves to thank. We are now reaping what we ourselves have sown."

Such are the words of a profound thinker who, to his fame as a thinker, adds a parallel fame of piety. Amid some of the unparalleled doctrines of our Church arose the intellectual revolt of the present times, and we can only check the progress of the evil by withdrawing the cause. It is an ominous fact that the liberal creed which the charges in this case so attack has sprung chiefly from that land which once lay wholly subject to the severe tenets of the Puritans.

It seems to me the world is now fully ready for an orthodoxy that shall firmly, yet tenderly, preach all of the creed except its plain errors or dark views of God and man. Not one of you, my brethren, has preached the dark theology of Jonathan Edwards in your whole life. Nothing could induce you to preach it, and yet it is written down in your creed in dreadful plainness. Confess, with me, that our beloved Church has slipped away from the religion of despair, and has come unto Mount Sion, into the atmosphere of Jesus as He was in life and in death, full of love and forgiveness. And yet it is only in the narrow field just pointed out that I have in any way departed from the doctrines of the Presbyterian Church.

One of the most distinguished of our theological teachers in the East has written: "There is not enough in the indictment to convict one of heresy. All these commotions only point to a time when sectarianism will disappear, and all Christians will meet on the platform of a common faith in one Christ and one Savior, and, fastening all their faith upon Him as a Redeemer, will cast off many of the forms which now perplex them."

Beloved brethren, I, holding the general creed as rendered by the former New School Theologians, I will, in addition to such a general statement, repeat to you articles of belief upon which I am willing to meet the educated world, and the skeptical world, and the sinful world, using my words in the evangelical sense: The inspiration of the Holy Scriptures, the Trinity, the divinity of Christ, the office of Christ as a mediator when grasped by an obedient faith, conversion by God's spirit, man's natural sinfulness, and the final separation of the righteous and wicked.

I have now read before you an outline of my public method and of my Christian creed. It is for you to decide whether there is in me orthodox belief sufficient to retain me in your brotherhood. Having confessed everywhere that the value of a single life does not depend upon sectarian relations, but upon evangelical or Christian relations, I am perfectly willing to cross a boundary which I have often shown to be narrow; but, going from you, if such be your order at last, it is the evangelical Gospel I shall still preach, unless my mind should pass through undreamed of changes in the future.

From the prosecutor of this case I would not withhold my conviction that he has acted from a sense of duty; therefore, to him and to you all, brethren, I extend good-will, and hope that in a wisdom religious and fraternal you will be enabled to do what is right in the sight of God.

Yours, with love, DAVID SWING.

www.ingramcontent.com/pod-product-compliance
Lightning Source LLC
LaVergne TN
LVHW021411110826
845150LV00007B/1869

9781425511296